DELILAH

and Others Like Her

Pet owners sharing their joys,
responsibilities and sorrows, showing
unconditional love is a two-way street.

Trish Titus

Independence, Missouri

DELILAH and Others Like Her
Copyright © 2019 by Trish Titus

All rights reserved. Printed in the United States of America. No part of this book may be used or reproduced in any manner whatsoever without written permission.

Please write to the author at Tmtpetstories18@gmail.com.

- Permission granted by each and every contributor for their story and photo(s).
- Permission granted by Crystal E. Henze from San Antonio, Texas for use of her rooster photo.
- Permission granted by Animal Shelters and Rescue Leagues to provide their names and information.
- Permission granted by Pet Loss Support Groups to provide their names and information.

Cover and interior design: Trish Titus
Editing: Stephanie Fleming
Graphic Designer: Rebecca Shaw, BrockleyDesigns.com

Library of Congress Control Number: 2018908608

ISBN (978-1-7323352-0-2) (Ebook-EPUB)
ISBN (978-1-7323352-1-9) (Paperback)
ISBN (978-1-7323352-2-6) (Ebook-MOBI)

Acknowledgments

Amber McCarty, Kathy B., Ann Fulk,
Stephanie Fleming, Elizabeth Redford,
Connie Niemeyer, Kath Schroeder, Dan Grade,
Ray McCarty, Carol Miller, Lori Grade,
Marcia Olson, Shawn Wolf, Janie Williams,
Geno Grade, Hannah Hubert, Debbie Scott,
Kris Scott and Jeremy Scott

To each and every one of my contributors, I want to say a big Thank You. You were open and willing to share your memories, the joys, delights and responsibilities, as well as the pain and sadness of losing your incredible pets. I can only imagine the kind of lives they had with you and your families, and what they truly meant to you.

To Stephanie Fleming, thank you for your editing skills and questions for my contributors to help bring out their stories.

To Rebecca Shaw, my graphic designer, thank you for bringing your expertise to the table in shaping up the flow for easy reading and refining the interior. I couldn't have done it without you.

Thank you to all the Animal Shelters & Rescue Leagues for allowing me to list your facilities. I hope this will bring you the support needed for all those wonderful animals you take in and love and care for until their forever homes become available, as well as whatever you need for your facilities that you continue to do this work for a long time. I also hope this will help more people find their way to you to help volunteer in whatever capacity is needed. Animals of all kinds need our unconditional love and support. We are the only voice they have.

Thank you to the Pet Loss Support Groups for allowing me to list your facilities. After losing a pet, we sometimes become lost ourselves. So many different thoughts flood our minds, how do we go home, they aren't there. Home feels empty and quiet without them. What do we do with their bowls and food, beds and toys, etc. Many times family and friends aren't able to provide the support needed to help get us through the grieving process, especially if they've never owned a pet. It's like, they just don't get it. These pets are like our kids. I hope that if any pet owners need support, or a shoulder to lean and cry on, that they have the courage to reach out to you and ask for help.

Thank you, Holly Yandle *(Out of The Tunnels of PTSD)*. Holly was my former accountability buddy. She told me to never give up and keep going; it's not a race.

To Roe Irlbeck, my good friend and former co-worker. Thank you for always giving me your honest opinion when I asked for your help. I have always trusted your judgment.

And to you the reader, thank you for taking the time to read these wonderful stories. If you had a pet pass away, I'm sorry for your loss. My hope is that these memories that have been shared, will bring you some comfort knowing that you are not alone in the grieving process, and that just maybe, they brought a little light into your life.

In Memory Of

Delilah

Mick

Jersey

Nikki

Ripple

Cisco

ChiChi

Heidi

Hershey

Tanjie

Laddie

Mozart

Jefé

Buddy & Dante

Prince

Winnie

Tootsie

Chaddy Noody

Abby

Epigraph

"A journey of a thousand miles must begin with a single step."

Lao-Tzu, ancient Chinese philosopher

Contents

Acknowledgments ~ iii

In Memory Of ~ v

Epigraph ~ vii

Contents ~ ix

Preface ~ xi

Introduction ~ xiii

Delilah ~ 15

Mick ~ 31

Jersey ~ 35

Nikki ~ 41

Ripple ~ 45

Cisco ~ 51

ChiChi ~ 55

Heidi ~ 67

Hershey ~ 73

Tanjie Cat Miller ~ 81

Laddie ~ 85

Mozart ~ 93

Jefé ~ 97

Buddy & Dante ~ 111

Prince ~ 117

Winnie ~ 121

Tootsie ~ 127

Chaddy Noody ~ 131

Abby ~ 135

Animal Shelters and Rescue Leagues ~ 149

Pet Loss Resources ~ 161

How to Share Your Pet's Story ~ 165

About the Author ~ 167

Thoughts And Memory Pages ~ 169

Preface

For about a week after I put Delilah to sleep, I found myself looking at photos of her, tears rushing down my cheeks. I started writing down my memories of her because I didn't want to forget her or how she came to be with us. Then I thought why couldn't I share my thoughts and feelings of Delilah with others? What if I wrote a story about her. There were little details I had almost forgotten that I didn't think I would, but writing about her seemed to help me keep her memory alive. It was as if she was sitting there next to me, and I was telling someone about her.

What if other people were willing to open up and share memories of their beloved pets? Would they share their joys and responsibilities that go along with loving these animals? What was the relationship between them like, and would they share the sadness of losing their pet? I didn't want Delilah to be forgotten. I wanted her story, to live on, to showcase the unconditional love that we all share with these amazing animals, and why we call them family. I knew others would want to tell theirs as well.

Preface

The stories that fill these pages tell how they came to be with their forever families. Lessons learned by their humans in patience, kindness, respect and love, along with learning not to take life so seriously. If you've ever loved a pet, you'll recognize many of the same delights and duties of "pethood" that these people have shared, as well as the sorrows of losing them. But writing it down can help.

Delilah, you will always be in my heart.

Trish Titus

Introduction

Delilah and Others Like Her are memoirs from pet owners whose animals have passed away. They share what it was like adapting to having a pet join their family. When tragedy strikes a pet down, the pain is unbearable, or when a trip to the vet is necessary and the outcome is not what was expected, the denial and grieving process has started. Heartbreaking decisions are made.

My journey began with the loss of my sweet Delilah in October 2016. I wondered how I would make it through the day without her. How could I come home expecting her to greet me, but knowing that I would never see her again.

I didn't want Delilah to be forgotten. Writing down my memories of her helped with the grieving. It was a way to share her life.

I wondered if others had coped with their loss any better than I had. I wanted to know and share their stories. Each chapter is someone telling the story of their beloved pet.

Are you one of the millions of owners who has grieved a pet? If so, I am very sorry for your loss. I know what it feels like.

You are not alone in this journey. Neither are we.

Here are our stories.

DELILAH
Iowa/Missouri

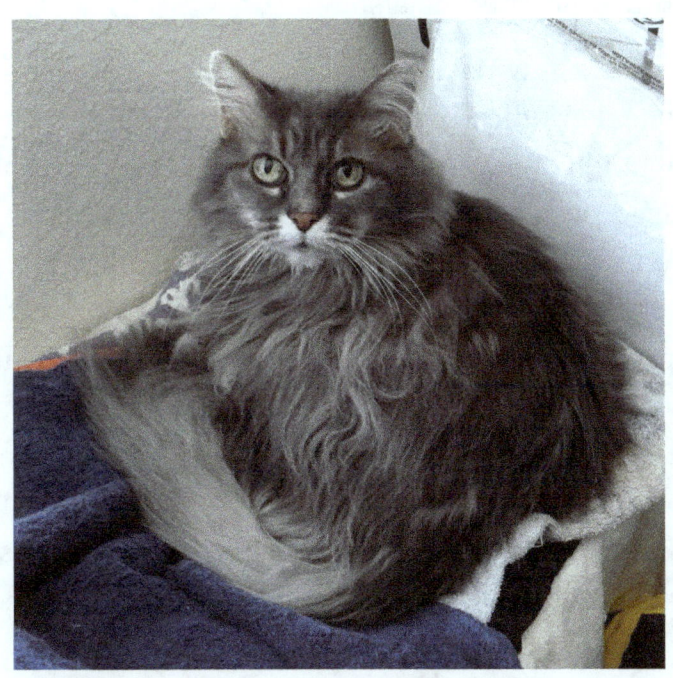

Unknown – October 28, 2016

DELILAH

It's July 2007. Had we been five minutes earlier or five minutes later pulling up in the driveway, we may not have seen her. She was in the shadow of the air conditioner, low on the ground and in her mouth a baby bunny. I remember after stopping the car, my daughter opened her door to get out and walked slowly towards this little furry feline. The kitty stopped dead in her tracks looking at us with the wiggling bunny. My daughter told her quite profoundly to "Put that baby bunny down, or Karma will come and get you!" It wasn't more than a few seconds, and she dropped the bunny still looking at my daughter while the rabbit made a fast getaway, and within moments she also ran.

Over the next few days, we saw this kitty hanging around our house. Periodically she would hide underneath my car so she wouldn't get wet; it had been raining for several days. We noticed she also would hide under our front porch which was open and dry. Little by little over the next few weeks she started hanging around more often. We would be sitting on the steps of our porch, and she would come and walk up one or two steps. We could pet her, and she seemed to be okay with that. One day my daughter was sitting on a lawn chair near the front porch, and the kitty jumped up into her lap startling her. My daughter wasn't sure whether she should pet her or not but after a few moments, she did, and the kitty just sat there enjoying it.

We lived next door to my dad, the house I grew up in with both my parents and my siblings. My mom passed away in January 2006. One day my dad looked out his bedroom window and saw us with the kitty, so he came over to talk with us; she perked her ears up and looked at him. As he got closer and started to bend over to pet her, she jumped off my daughter's lap and ran away.

She started coming around more often walking up the porch steps and sitting on the top step, the porch had a slight overhang, and she sat as close to the door as she could. One day it was raining heavily, we were sitting inside the enclosed porch and heard a meow. We looked out the window, and there she sat at the top of the steps trying not to get wet. We opened the door, and in she came. Well, there we sat and here she sat, wet.

She looked thin. I went to get a small bowl of water and a towel to dry her and as she drank the water my daughter said, "You know you're going to be feeding her soon and then she'll be inside." I looked at her with a slight frown and said "No I'm not; I'm just going to give her some water." Well, after that I did give her more water, and I started providing her with little bits of kitty food that I bought and then she was coming around more often. OK, so I gave in. She started staying in the house at night, and then we let her out in the morning not knowing for sure if she would come back, but she did. As we got into fall, the weather was getting much colder. She seemed to be more comfortable and content with us and was happy just staying inside.

A couple of times when we would pick her up she would give a little cry as it hurt towards her backside, so we needed to be gentle. When she came to us, there was no collar, so we

DELILAH

didn't have a name for her or any indication as to who she belonged to. I didn't post a picture of her. I got to thinking that maybe someone had mistreated her and they might continue or maybe they were just glad to be rid of her, but I really didn't know that either.

We wanted to name her. My daughter started to call her Mrs. Norris for a short while, after the cat in *Harry Potter*, who she resembled somewhat, being thin. She didn't want us to continue calling her that so we eventually came up with the name Delilah.

It was the summer of 2009 after my daughter graduated from high school, and went to college, that I had to move in with my dad next door. The little house we were living in was no longer safe. Once we were in my dad's house which was a two-story house, Delilah now had lots of rooms to roam around in and space to be adventurous. Over time, she warmed up to my dad and was fine.

I was always very grateful when I would come home from work, and she would be sitting at the top of the stairs leading to the upper living room waiting for me. She seemed to know when I would get home. Dad would make comments that he could come in from outside and she wouldn't give him the time of day. She knew the sound of my car from at least a half block away and was always there at the top of the stairs waiting for me. I would walk through the front door putting my things down, pick her up and the purring would start and I loved that.

I had a bunch of plastic, colored Easter eggs that I would place on the floor as toys. I wasn't sure she'd even play with them. She would soon bat them around and chase them, and I would giggle. My bedroom was upstairs, and I had taken a lot of the eggs upstairs with me. Several times after playing with the eggs they would get close to the top of the stairs. She would give one of those eggs a little swat and watch it bounce down only to go chasing after it. The egg would hit the bottom of the step possibly landing in a shoe or some container, and there she would sit looking at it and then up at me as if to say "OK, come down here and get it out for me so I can do it again." I'd go down and retrieve it throwing it up the stairs and watch her scamper up to find it. It was so fun to watch her play as she would squat down, wiggling her back end before darting towards the colored eggs and scatter them around.

There were times during the night that she would come up on the bed and lay down on my chest, whether that was because she thought I snored too loudly and hoped it would stop, or that she just wanted to be close to me. After about five or six minutes she'd move over to one of the pillows which I had covered with an old towel, or to the open window sill and go to sleep.

I lived in my dad's house for a good five plus years with Delilah. After my daughter graduated from Iowa State University in 2013, she then went through a one year post baccalaureate program. I helped her move to the State of Kansas to be with her fiancé the summer of 2014. By the fall of 2014, my job ended, and I had to start looking for a new one. It wasn't long when my daughter asked me to move closer to where she lived. I eventually found a job and moved after the first of the year in 2015. I would be staying with her and my future son-in-law until I could find a place of my own. It was several weeks before I was able to rent an apartment which would be closer to my job on the Missouri side. I could now move some of my belongings, including Delilah, down with me from Iowa. She stayed with my dad while I was looking for a place to live. I missed her so much, but finally, she was with me.

We moved in on a Sunday. I had to go to work the next day, Monday, and leave Delilah all by herself among the boxes and totes with her toys, food and kitty litter box and other familiar items from back home. I felt guilty leaving her by herself in a strange new place, nowhere near as big as the house we lived in, and now there were new smells and new sounds. I missed her during the day, so as soon as I got home from work, I put everything down, picked her up and held her, telling her about my day. I would sit on the floor with her, talking to her, and she would stretch out as I brushed her all over especially her belly and armpits. She played with her colored eggs, chasing them around. Periodically I would step on one of those colored eggs and oops, another egg bit the dust.

It was sometime in early August 2016, my daughter had come over to my place, and she noticed that Delilah was drooling and said we ought to get her checked out. I knew she hadn't been feeling well, so I made the appointment to take her to the vet with my daughter coming with me. They examined Delilah noting a heart murmur which we already knew from our vet in Iowa; as well as having had a couple UTI's (Urinary Tract Infections). The vet also noted that one of Delilah's kidneys seemed abnormal and possibly not functioning well. She was also seeing periodontal disease. Then she said there was a small growth under Delilah's tongue and showed me a picture which she took on her cellphone. It was strange to see this growth, imagine having a little knot or marble under your tongue. The vet said she thought it was possibly a "squamous cell carcinoma." Right off we didn't like that. This veterinarian preferred not to be the one to do anything with the growth. She told us we should see an internal vet and see what our options were.

So I made the appointment to see an internal vet that they recommended. My daughter came over so that we could take Delilah together as I didn't want to do this on my own. We arrived at the clinic feeling nervous about what might take place. After they examined Delilah, she was put back in her carry case, and then we were taken to a small waiting room where the vet visited with us providing us with a couple of options; we found we didn't like any of them. A decision needed to be made, so we decided to go ahead that day with the aspiration on this thing under Delilah's tongue.

With Delilah still in her carry case, a vet tech carried her back through some doors. We sat in the same waiting room and waited for the vet to come back and talk with us about the upcoming procedure. I was feeling nervous, and I could feel my heart beating a little more quickly. I tried to remain calm as I didn't want my daughter to see how scared I really was. The vet handed me a clipboard with some papers on it for my signature, one of the last sheets was a DNR (Do Not Resuscitate) sheet. We knew what that meant, and we both broke down and cried. The thought of losing her that day scared us. We weren't ready or prepared for that to happen, but we felt we had to do something to try to help Delilah. We hoped that she would be alright. The vet told us she was pretty sure Delilah would be okay going under for the aspiration, but needed to have a decision made…so I signed the papers.

We waited for almost a good hour while they did the procedure and then waited for Delilah to recover for about another hour before we were able to take her home later that day. That was September 15th, my Birthday.

The test results came back from the specialty lab in Arizona within a week. The report said there was no definitive diagnosis. I thought "why can't you provide us with something, is it benign or is it cancerous." After the vet went over the report with me, she gave me some other options for treatment which I would have to inform my daughter. I didn't like any of those.

A little over a week later we decided to go for a second aspiration. The vet was going to try to get a larger tissue sample from under Delilah's tongue. I would take her back to this same internal vet before heading to work and pick her up later in the afternoon. I was told Delilah was to have NO food or water after midnight. That was the worst feeling knowing I would have to pick up both of her bowls. My heart sank. I lost my appetite to eat thinking if Delilah wasn't going to be able to eat or drink anything, then I was going to have to be careful not to eat in front of her, and have her look at me like "Why are you eating and drinking, but you picked up my bowls, and I don't get to eat or drink!" It made me sad. I felt like she might think I was punishing her for something and of course, that wasn't the case at all, but trying to tell an animal you can't have food or water... well, it sucks.

Several times throughout the night, she came into my bedroom meowing at me. All I could do was to keep telling her I'm sorry, and how much I loved her, and that she was going to have to wait until after her appointment with the vet like she was going to understand a single thing I said. I can't imagine what she may have been thinking.

It's September 29th; I took her in before heading to the office, I hated leaving her there. I felt nervous and anxious throughout the day about how she was doing and wondering if she was OK. I left work early and headed back to the animal hospital to pick her up. I was told she did well, which was a relief. We headed home and once out of her carry case she went straight to the kitchen. I wondered if they had given her any food or water, she acted like she hadn't eaten for days. I called them, and no, they hadn't as that was a medical liability.

The aspirated sample was once again sent to the same specialty lab down in Arizona for testing. I didn't know why it had to go all the way down there; I didn't think to ask, but I wish I would have. I was really hoping this time for a better, more definitive answer when the test result would come back. Another week went by and finally the test results came back, and once again there was no conclusive diagnosis. I thought, "You've got to be kidding me!" I was very unhappy with no answer whether Delilah had cancer or not. I didn't understand why they couldn't give us any kind of answer. Wasn't there enough tissue to work with? Once again the internal vet went through a couple of things with me which I would relay to my daughter. We could try one final aspiration or we could take her to another specialty vet over in Overland Park, Kansas for surgery to remove the growth. The cost would be in the ballpark of $1500.00 to $1800.00, and still not know whether she would survive it, or we could try a new medication which "might" shrink the tumor, but it was no guarantee.

About a week later we decided to give the medication a try. Delilah was still having a lot of difficulty eating and drinking; she was sleeping a lot more and not urinating or pooping much. Trying to get the medication in her was even harder, more of it got on me rather than in her.

She would wake me at various times throughout the night wanting to eat something and drink water. I tried everything that I knew to help her eat and drink, I knew she was also trying, but not much was going in or coming out. I would hold her and walk with her like you would when your child is sick. She was losing weight; drooling more and wasn't able to bathe herself anymore like kitties are supposed to. Her fur was becoming more matted. Delilah was looking quite poorly. She used to love getting brushed, but now she didn't like it as I'm sure it hurt even though I was trying to be so gentle.

I believe she possibly suffered two little seizures or what I thought may have been seizures. I was able to catch her so she wouldn't fall over during these episodes and hurt herself; I felt her heart racing as I lay her gently down on the floor. It scared me, and I could feel the tears coming as I thought why is this happening to her. The episodes lasted for a few moments or so and then she seemed to be OK and would get up and walk away. She was sleeping a lot more, didn't greet me at the door like she used to, and all I could do was think this wasn't fair to her or us. I would watch her sleep so peacefully and through tears had a hard time imagining her not with me.

I knew she was slipping away from us, and I couldn't let her keep suffering. I knew that I was going to have to make the tough decision to let her go and I hated it more than I can say.

To make this decision, I felt like someone knocked the wind out of me and I couldn't breathe.

Delilah before she got sick.

I was going to have to be the one to say when it was time to let her go, and I felt the time had now come. I was going to have to tell my daughter that I just couldn't watch her suffer any longer. Delilah had lived with me for nine long years. She was there for me, and I wasn't ready for this. What was I going to do without her? My daughter had said when we first took Delilah into the specialty internal vet that rather than have her suffer "*Letting her go, would be the kindest thing we could do for her.*" As hard as it would be and as much as we loved her, those words came back to me now. I called my daughter and through tears told her it's time, I couldn't do this anymore, it was too hard to continue watching this beautiful little girl of ours suffer. It wasn't fair to her.

Friday evening, October 28, 2016, my daughter came over, we had to get Delilah out from underneath a chair and put her in her carry case. We know animals can't talk to us so that we understand what they are feeling or their thoughts, but, oh how I wished with all my heart that she could have told us that she knew what was happening. That it was OK and it was her time to go or to stop, that she was going to be OK, and she didn't need to go anywhere, but to be with me for a while longer. But, we took her to our original veterinarian where we had a little more time with her. Guilt had been creeping up on me. I signed the papers, and they took her to the back where they would put her to sleep. To say that royally sucked was an understatement.

The tears wouldn't quit for either my daughter or me. Part of me wished I had gone back with them and held Delilah and petted her when they put her to sleep so she wouldn't be alone, (my biggest regret now) but then part of me couldn't bear to watch her pass away. My daughter couldn't bear to go back with them, and I was thinking I needed to be with her at that moment. I continue to feel torn about my decision regarding that day, and still feel guilty with all kinds of "what if's." I've had good days, and bad days, they are slowly getting better. The tears still come. I didn't want her remains discarded or dumped in some pile, so we had her cremated, and she's with me, only in a different form. All I can say is that we both miss her terribly and love her still so much.

I happened to watch a spider cross my kitchen floor one day and got to thinking about how Delilah was my bug watcher, that's how I knew I had some of those in my home. She would sit and watch them, and, as if she would answer me, I would say "Delilah, what are you looking at?", if I didn't see it. She would barely glance up at me as if to say "If I take my eyes off that thing with legs it will move and then you can't kill it." Sometimes she would slowly walk behind a bug or beside it so as not to lose sight of it and then I would have that opportunity to, well, you know what happens. I miss my bug-watcher.

I am so grateful that we had her for those nine plus years. I'm not ready just yet to get another pet, even though there are so many who need safe and loving homes, I know mine will be when the time comes. Delilah is not the first pet I've had in my life. My siblings and I grew up with a dog, her name was Heidi, and her story is also in this book.

For anyone who is thinking about getting a pet, please be responsible about it. Do your research so you know and understand what it means to own a pet no matter the size or breed. If you can, please rescue and adopt. Remember, they are not a toy or a novelty thing that you can forget and toss aside after having grown tired of its presence. This is a big deal; they become your family member. You need to take care of them as you would yourself or your children. If you wouldn't allow something to happen to you or to your child, don't allow it to happen to your pet. They depend on you; you're their total world, their guardians. It is a big decision to make, but know that the reward of having them in your life is also big. They provide comfort, joy, and companionship, as well as provide health benefits. What you give to them will come back to you. Make sure you give them your very best; your "unconditional love."

Trish Titus

Delilah taught me to slow down, be patient and enjoy those moments to sit quietly with her, and let the worries of the day pass.

Life is too short to be scared, upset or angry.

MICK
Missouri

1990 – 2004

MICK

My mother, pictured above, had loved, treasured and adored this dog so much when she was alive. She was heartbroken when he passed away.

My brother, Loren, and I found him wandering the back roads out by Lake Kernodle, Missouri. He was limping down the hot, dusty road with a choker collar wrapped around his neck, and leg causing him to have only three legs to walk on. He was an absolute pitiful sight. I pulled my car over and hopped out to free him from the choker when suddenly he jumped into my car. After a few unsuccessful tries to coax him from my car, my brother and I shrugged and headed home with him. He was having the time of his life on the ride home, hanging his head out the window, tongue lapping up the wind wearing a huge grin on his face.

When we got home, mother informed us we needed to find his home ASAP; surely someone was missing this beautiful dog. The next day she called the lake's office and the vet's office to inquire if anyone was missing a pet. She made fliers and posted them all around the area. Mother wasn't upset that we brought him home because one of us was always bringing home strays in need of rescue. But with this dog, she was firm that if his owner wasn't located, he couldn't live at our house. As the days passed, and no owner found, she grew more attached to him, so he became a part of our family from that point on. He never left.

My mother named him Mick after the lead singer of *The Rolling Stones*, Mick Jagger. She had confused Mick Jagger for another singer David Bowie who most people thought had two different colored eyes. David Bowie, at about age fifteen, suffered a terrible injury to his left eye. His best buddy caused this and over a girl. But, our Mick had one ice-blue eye and one hazel eye.

Mick lived a very happy life with my mother until the day he passed away from bone cancer. They would go on daily nature walks, do yoga, hang out and sing music together. My mother would sing while playing guitar or the piano and Mick would howl his tune. Mother wrote many poems about pets, family, friends, and nature in general. She wrote the poem included with this story and drew a little picture of him lounging on his bed. She adored her Mickydo as she fondly called him.

Amber McCarty

MICK

A Gentle Soul

A gentle soul with questing eyes,
- One tiger gold one glacial blue -
Imagines in a dreamy sleep,
He's chasing after Caribou.
In loping strides, he kicks up snow,
Slips sideways after fleeing feet,
Glides steady over icy straight,
Builds speed before his final leap.
Waking with a puzzled start
He sniffs the air with wistful snout,
Expels a disappointed "Uff,"
Drops husky mask to quiet foot.

RLE – September 1, 2000

JERSEY
Iowa

May 20, 2007 - December 22, 2016

JERSEY

She came into our family on July 4, 2008. My son, Jason, and I went to Farnhamville, Iowa to see a Dachshund dog that was for sale listed in the newspaper. This family had gotten her as a puppy from a breeder in Story City, Iowa. We learned she was born on May 20th, 2007, and that she was a registered Dachshund. The current owners had named her Jersey. She didn't fit in well with their family, and they continually scolded her. Jersey was small; a seven pound dappled red dog. She was a bit deformed with one eye smaller than the other, and one smaller nostril that made her wheeze at times, thus the nickname–Wheezy.

Jersey was our first house dog, and we adapted well. She loved everyone, and every animal she ever met became her friend, to her anyway. Jersey was a bit of a hyper dog and also loved to jump on the couch to sleep in a corner with a blanket. She looked forward to car rides, often jumping on the center console trying to stand on her back legs to see out. When she saw an animal, she'd bark like crazy as if to say, hey, let's be friends! She loved to stand on her back legs to beg for food, pets, everything.

Jersey loved to eat and was very food motivated. There were only two foods she didn't like - mushrooms and onions. She had a dribbling problem and would tinkle every time she got excited, which was often. We would take her on walks with our two outside dogs; she loved going along for those walks.

The fall of 2010, we noticed she was having problems and would be shaking when we finished with our walks as if she was hurting and getting stiff. After a trip to the vet, he put her on medication which seemed to help. The vet suggested getting a puppy in the house to keep her moving; they felt it would be beneficial to her so, in October 2010, we did get another Dachshund and named her Sadie Sue.

Jersey in front, Sadie Sue in back.

Jersey was on and off medications the whole next year, so her walking days were over. The drug would help at times, but not always. In March 2011, Jersey was in more and more pain. The limp in her right back leg was getting worse, she was dragging it more than walking and her tail wasn't able to wag much either. On March 23, she was hardly able to move at all. Keeping her kenneled and on meds just wasn't the answer any longer. I called a different veterinarian; one who we had heard was starting to do back surgeries locally. He wanted to see her right away. It sounded like she was a good candidate for him.

The doctor took x-rays; he wanted to do all he could for her. She was to have surgery that night. He was going to do whatever it took, hoping she was strong enough to survive and heal without the use of a doggie wheelchair.

The surgery took an hour, and she had eighteen staples down her back. Remember, she was a small dog. She stayed at the vets for the next two weeks. I went to visit her every day, doing water therapy with her and feeding her. Jersey had a few complications, but her strong will came out through it all. The doctor always thought her deformities might have had something to do with her problems since her problems were unusual for such a young dog. The prior family may have mistreated her. Maybe she was kicked? Our vet discussed this with us, and we learned about how it can have effects later in life.

Jersey was still a "loving everyone" kind of dog. No matter how tough life was, she just loved everyone. Everyone around her understood her problem and could handle her as well as help her up and down the steps, or they would hold her, which Jersey loved. She had to be held up when sitting on her back end, or it bothered her back too much. I got her a puppy carrier so she could go along for walks and I could carry her around a long time that way.

We lived with her bathroom messes and no more walks. We'd help her up and down a step at a time due to her back leg not working the way it was supposed to. She did learn how to get into a run outside so she could get where she wanted to, and she could move pretty quickly. She loved to go outside. She lived her way until other problems started coming up with more frequency, resulting in worse bathroom problems.

In 2016, Jersey was diagnosed with IBS (Irritable Bowel Syndrome), with more medications. By November 2016, she couldn't control anything anymore. Her eating had slowed way down. By December, we realized just how much she was failing. Her attitude never changed. Jersey always wanted to be petted and be around family. But now all she wanted was to lie down on her bed. She wasn't eating much of anything. Losing weight while her stomach was getting bigger and her backbone was protruding. Things were not going well.

We decided that Jersey didn't need to suffer any longer just because we were not ready to say goodbye. Saying goodbye to my little girl was the hardest thing I ever did. On December 22, 2016, I held her in my arms, getting a last kiss as she went to sleep.

Jersey was always loved, and she crossed the bridge quietly. I know now she is happy and running as she did as a puppy. No more pain. No more medications. She now has lots of friends.

Run free my little Jersey.

Kathy B.

What Jersey taught me was love.
She loved everyone no matter how she felt.
She simply wanted attention and gave back way more.

NIKKI

Missouri

1997 - May 2011

NIKKI

I picked out this little girl at a breeder's home. She was just a puppy, at ten weeks old. She was a beautiful silver color with blue eyes. I chose her because I loved Huskies as a breed, and mostly for me. But, I was more than willing to share her with my family; I also owned three cats.

I've always loved the name Nikki, so that was the name I gave her. Nikki had a wonderful personality; she was so sweet and yet had an ornery side to her. She was groomed regularly and would periodically break loose and run all over the clinic.

We boarded her one time, and when we picked her up, her report card stated that she was the class clown. So, she must have had a good time.

Nikki never traveled with us. When it came to other people visiting our home, she was terrific. We always said she would lick a burglar on his way out.

She started having trouble with her hips when she was about twelve and a half years old. It was difficult for her to get around. She weighed about eighty-six pounds. It was May 2011, when we decided to put her down due to health issues; it was such a sad and terrible day for all of us, me especially. She was two weeks shy of being fourteen.

I knew the next dog I would get had to be small and not shed. It would need to get along with children. It was about a year and a half before we got another dog. This time we went to an animal shelter. Gretta was her name; she was a Schnauzer. Gretta had been a stray who was picked up in Hutchinson, Kansas and taken to a shelter called Wayside Waifs.

Hutchinson had a kill shelter. We are very thankful that both Hutchinson and Salina would bring dogs to Wayside Waifs.

I feel that anyone who is thinking about buying or adopting a pet should check out the breed carefully. I would say go to any animal shelters and rescue centers first and find out if they will be the right choice for you and your family. So many pets need good, clean, safe and loving homes. They will show you unconditional love; they don't know any other way.

Ann Fulk

Nikki taught me how to be more loving to all.

RIPPLE
Wisconsin/Kansas

2011 - 2014

I had just graduated college from UNL in Nebraska and moved up to Madison, Wisconsin to be with my mom during foot surgery. When I arrived I had two hamsters with me: Darcy and Scallop, two different dwarves, one was terrified of people, and the other was a mean biter. Within the first week of the move, I was getting lonely, mom was at work all day while I was waiting for foot surgery; I still had months to go before operations would start. I had seen a pet shop while driving around and discovered that they had Syrian hamsters: they were larger and friendlier than the hamsters I had. Even though I lacked a lot of space, I brought Ripple home.

Initially, mom wasn't enthused. I had already brought two hamsters home, and that was a lot, but she quickly fell in love with Ripple. He was super tiny and delicate. It turns out he was very sick, and we thought he would die. I wasn't having it. I'd gotten to three hamsters to find one that liked me. I gave him over-the-counter medicine (wet-tail drops), this is a liquid treatment. Wet tail is a stress-induced diarrhea that is very debilitating in hamsters and often fatal. Besides the drops, I also gave him Pedialyte for hydration and Karo Syrup to increase his appetite. These were suggestions I found online. He had become great about taking medication from a dropper, and he loved the syrup. I put it on my finger once, and he nipped me over it. I would then place it on a spoon, and he tried nipping that, he never nipped again. You could hold the smallest crumb in your hand, and he would daintily pick it out instead of nipping.

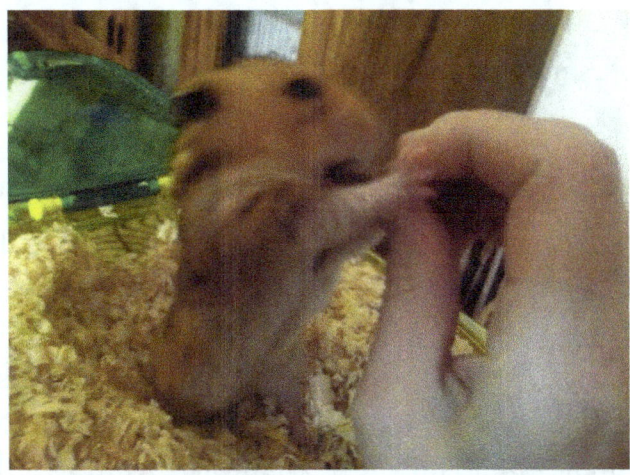

Since I was new to Wisconsin, and mostly housebound, I didn't get to meet many people or make friends. As cheesy as it sounds, Ripple kept me company. He would trail after me and my crutches in his ball and would nap on my mom's lap at night. He'd crawl up on his cage door and rattle the bars to be let out; it was like he'd figured out we paid attention to the noise.

One night, after surgery, when I was medicated with heavy painkillers, I forgot to close his cage door. Around 1:00 a.m. my mother came to get me, a medicated invalid with one working leg, out of bed. Ripple had climbed up and over stacks of books in her room and had gotten himself trapped. She was certain he would bite her out of fear and panic. I leaned down on one leg into the corner and plucked him up without issue.

Because of his learning not to bite, he became an excellent tool for families with small children. Parents in Wisconsin and Kansas City, when I moved down to the KC area, would bring small children to my home to learn how to handle a small pet safely.

Please remember that during my surgery I was *heavily* medicated. Wisconsin was in the middle of Governor Scott Walker's recall election. As a result, I formatted a theoretical hamster campaign against Walker. I gave Ripple political ideals and catchphrases. He would "rattle the cages of our oppressors," he was for assisting Syrian refugees, as a Syrian himself. He was a strong environmentalist who recycled toilet paper tubes and used them as furniture around his home. I was on some powerful painkillers.

Many people view anything other than a standard dog or cat as a lesser pet; one we let die because they're inexpensive. Ripple, to me, was an irreplaceable hamster. He came down with me to Kansas City towards a toxic relationship when I had no one else.

Stephanie and Ripple

While I was strong enough to leave for myself, I left more urgently for Ripple. My ex would throw things, throw temper tantrums, and act out aggressively. It terrified me he would one-day chuck Ripple. One night it got far too close. I called a friend and moved the last of my belongings AND Ripple out of the apartment and into our new home.

He lived about a year longer and was there with me through job searches, medical issues, good days, and bad days. Ripple was great at snuggling and scooting around in his ball all over the place. Eventually, he passed away because of a problem with his digestive tract. We tried to have him treated; but the veterinarian could only do so much.

He was incredibly special to me. It simply hasn't been possible to consider another pet; a hamster or any other animal. I'm lucky to have had the little fluff ball for as long as I did.

Stephanie Fleming

What I learned from Ripple was the value of small things.

CISCO

Wisconsin

Cisco being hugged by big brother Buttermilk

1998 - 2015

Cisco was one of our family cats growing up, but I always felt he was my own. I was the one who picked him out. My mom, brother, two sisters, and I were at church camp that summer. My dad couldn't be at camp due to work, so it was just the five of us.

I remember one day wandering the camp with my older sister when we found an old horse barn. It was near the edge of camp, yet far enough away from most of the activity. We were wandering through the barn when we heard little mews coming from a feeding box full of hay. We saw a litter of kittens. Some kittens were in the box, and some were playing in the different stalls. One particularly playful kitten had caught my eye, a little orange tabby with a notched ear, he came right over to say hello and kept playing. We fell in love with him and ran to tell our mom about him. We needed to see if she would let us keep him. According to mom, now wasn't the time to get another cat as we already had two at home, Denver and Buttermilk (Butter for short).

We were crushed and went to visit the kittens multiple times a day playing with all of them. During the last days of camp, I was talking to my dad on the phone about what we had been doing. I told him about finding the kitten and how much we wanted to keep him, when he said, "Put mom on the phone."

After a long conversation with my mom, she hung up the phone and said, "Okay, we can keep him." We were absolutely ecstatic and ran to get the kitten and find a box to put him in and take him home. My brother, Alex, had named him for the captain of *Deep Space Nine*; we were big *Star Trek* fans!

We held Cisco on our laps all the way; there were multiple fights about whose turn it was to hold him. When we finally arrived home, dad took us aside and said he needed to talk to us about something. He told us that the reason we could bring Cisco home was because our cat, Denver, had passed away while we were at camp. Denver was quite old and had died peacefully in his sleep. Our dad thought it would help the transition to bring a new cat into our lives with Denver's passing.

We were young at the time; I was around seven years old. We didn't understand the meaning of death, but we knew we couldn't see Denver anymore.

We could focus on the new kitten and got to enjoy watching him learn and grow. I only remember bits and pieces of him growing up now, but I do recall him being extremely playful with our older cat Butter. Cisco would hop around him wanting to play all the time while Butter just wanted to lay and rest. Butter was also a huge cat while Cisco was always a scrawny little thing. Seeing them sit next to each other was amusing due to their size differences. Our family usually had three to four cats at a time; it was unusual that we only had Butter (which we also called Grandpa Butter in his later years) and Cisco for almost ten years. They got along so well, sitting side by side at the window watching the birds and chattering amongst themselves.

Cisco never grew out of being a barn cat and did anything he could to get outside. He often sneaked out to hunt. He'd sit in the alley under my window when he was ready to come back in, and he'd cry until I woke up to let him inside. It was a special bond we had. I was the lightest sleeper, and somehow he knew which window to sit under so I would hear him. When I let him back in, he would often come and lay on my bed to sleep the rest of the night away.

Cisco lived a healthy seventeen years. Although he became a little stiff in later days, he was the same spirited cat throughout his whole life. We knew it was time to let him go when he could not keep any weight on and stopped eating. Although it was a difficult decision to make, we knew he had lived a good life, and hoped that he would pass peacefully. Although I have cats of my own now, I still remember him fondly as my "first kitty." I'll always have my favorite picture of the two of us. Me, a scrawny seven-year-old with missing teeth, and him, a scrawny kitten with a notched ear, happy to have found one another.

Elizabeth Redford

Cisco taught me to stay true to your roots and remember where you came from.

He was initially a wild barn cat.

He never lost his 'wild edge', and that was the most special and treasured thing about him.

CHICHI

Missouri

May 19, 2016 – May 2, 2017

CHICHI

My name is Connie Niemeyer, and my husband is Skip Niemeyer, and we are animal lovers. I don't have any children of my own, but Skip has three grown children. On May 2, 2017, we had six dogs and two turtles who are the receivers of most of our love, time and attention.

I am writing this from my bedroom where my remaining five furry love dogs surround me. I am very thankful that they are here with me. We could have easily lost all six of them that day, and that, I would not have survived.

We fostered Romeo, a Chihuahua whose owner had died. Romeo didn't like our other dogs, so although we loved him, we knew he was not a good fit. After having him for five months, we found an older couple with a Chiweenie, *a Chihuahua and Dachshund mix, adorably called either a Mexican Hotdog or German Taco*; I wanted a friend for their dog whose name was Pumpkin and hoped the two could be friends. During a play date, they got along so well I agreed to let them have Romeo even though I was nervous that neither dog had been spayed or neutered. Eventually, they had a litter of puppies.

We already had five rescue dogs and didn't need a puppy, but we loved Romeo and thought it would be nice to have one of his offspring. Pumpkin, the mother of the litter, had a mass on her breast and had to go into surgery when the puppies were only two weeks old. It was a miracle she and the puppies survived. They were under the care of a veterinarian until they turned six weeks old. That's the day I got to go to the vet and take the last tiny cinnamon-colored puppy home.

Her dad Romeo was a Chihuahua, and her mom Pumpkin was a Chiweenie. So for the first day we called her ChiChi Weenie, having a little more Chi in her. By the end of day one, we decided ChiChi was the perfect name for her.

ChiChi took three trips with us in her short life. Each time was a two-and-a-half hour drive to the Lake of the Ozarks. She was a perfect little travel mate and enjoyed all the attention she got from family and friends.

Unlike her dad, Romeo, whom we fostered for five months, ChiChi loved our other dogs! We have five dogs remaining, ranging from twelve pounds to fifty pounds. They came to us in various ways, and we are grateful for each of them.

ChiChi and Chewbacca

CHICHI

When we brought ChiChi home at six weeks old, she was only three pounds, but she was fearless! She ran circles around all of them, and loved playing tug of war with them. They had no shortage of stuffed chew toys, balls, and Frisbees; she loved them all. She was such a happy little dog.

ChiChi was a great swimmer from her first summer and beyond. We have many cute videos of her swimming. She was also the best at fetching her tennis ball, which was bigger than her head even though it was the small-sized ball! Her first toys were a little stuffed Chewbacca and an Ewok because we raised her to love *Star Wars*!

ChiChi was always fun and silly. When she was excited, she spun in circles which were the most adorable thing in the world! Of all of our dogs, she was the most cooperative with hats, costumes, and sweaters. The cutest was when she wore either her Kansas City Chiefs cheerleader dress or her Kansas City Chiefs jersey that our dog Molly outgrew. ChiChi was very photogenic.

Tragedy struck our canine family. We have a pool in our backyard and have always been very careful when the dogs are outside. We made sure that the dogs could swim and could easily find the stairs to get out. Living in Missouri, we would empty the pool for winter, and we kept the pool covered for the winter months. The cover was sturdy and could hold the weight of the dogs comfortably, but it was wearing out and was threadbare in spots. Last winter we threw out the pool cover, leaving the empty pool to collect leaves and dirt. This past spring we worked very hard cleaning it out, which may have given the dogs a false sense of security.

One morning, my husband decided it was warming up enough, and he turned on the hose where it sprinkled across the shallow end onto the slope leading down to the nine-foot-deep end of the pool. He didn't give it any more thought, and he left for work. I would leave about fifteen minutes later when I noticed the sprinkler aimed towards the pool. I wish I had followed my gut instinct. I went out to the back of the house and called my husband on the phone to see if it was a mistake or was he filling the pool now. He confirmed that he had turned it on to start filling the pool. I asked him if I should put something into the pool in case the dogs got in. He thought it would be okay, as I was only working a few hours that morning and at that point, the water hadn't even begun to accumulate. We hung up, and I stood there. I was kind of at a loss. I looked around for something to put in the deep end just in case, something for the dogs to stand on or climb on. I wish I had followed my original gut instinct and put something in the pool and not turning off that hose had become my biggest regret.

I left and headed to the hair salon where I help and worked my four hours. My full-time job is being a substitute teacher. After work, I had plans to take our dog Molly to the vet for routine shots and a checkup. My husband mentioned that I should wait until the next day, which was payday. Instead of going straight home I stopped to get gas and then went to McDonald's. I had planned to take Molly there for a hamburger patty after the vet, so I was craving it myself. Just as I got home, my husband texted that money was there and to take Molly to the vet.

Before giving the dogs their treats, which I always do when I come home from work, I get out of my work clothes and then I give them their treats. Monkey, Molly, Morgan, and Emily came, but no Sammy or ChiChi, which wasn't unusual. We have a doggy door, so I went out back and called for them with their treats in my hand when I heard splashing...

I ran to the pool and was horrified. My black Lab Sammy is splashing in a few feet of water, in the deep end; while my baby ChiChi, not even one-year-old yet, was floating on her side! I pulled off my shoes and threw my phone down. I ran across to the shallow end, and as I took my first step onto the slope, I slid down, like a water slide. I went all the way under, into the frigid cold water. As I stood up, my black Lab grabbed onto me and pulled me back down. I stood again; the water came to my chest, maybe three and a half feet deep by then. With Sammy clinging to me, I made my way over to

ChiChi. I held her upside down and squeezed water out of her. I started compressions and blew into her mouth and nose as I made my way to the slope. Then I realized we could not get out of the pool; the slope was steep and slippery. That's why the dogs were down there in the first place; they became entrapped in that cold water for god knows how long.

I was screaming between breaths and compressions. I was bawling because I was pretty sure I had lost ChiChi, but I kept giving her CPR (Cardiopulmonary Resuscitation). I'm not even sure how long that went on, it felt like a lifetime. As I yelled for help, finally a neighbor heard me screaming and came running to the fence. I gave her my garage code. When she entered the backyard, she threw a mat onto the slope, and I could push Sammy up to the mat so she could climb out. I was still holding my ChiChi and had my neighbor throw the hose in so I could pull myself out.

I was sure that ChiChi was gone, but I carried her inside, still bawling and called my husband. He told me to continue the compressions. I laid her on the couch and continued CPR while he stayed on the phone with me. I ran out the door as he pulled into the driveway and we rushed her to the vet just minutes away, but as I suspected, we were too late.

As traumatic as this was for us, all I think about is what my baby ChiChi went through; and Sammy too; who I believe went into the water after ChiChi to save her. Our hearts became shattered. My husband is heartbroken, and it weighs heavily on him. He blames himself as he was the one who decided to begin filling the pool that day and he regrets that decision. ChiChi was so special to my husband because his family had always leaned towards wiener dogs, which is probably a good part of the reason he had agreed to take her in.

ChiChi and Sammy

There are so many things we both could have done differently that day. What if I hadn't stopped for gas and McDonald's? What if I hadn't changed my clothes and used the bathroom? What if I had thrown a lawn chair in the pool that morning just in case? What if he had decided not to fill the pool until we were there to watch over it?

We love *all* of our dogs. Losing ChiChi this way was so shocking that it hurt more because she was so young. She didn't have the chance to live like our other pets have. We lost her due to drowning on May 2, 2017, two-and-a-half weeks before her first birthday on May 19th.

She was a nonstop bundle of love, playfulness, and cuddles. She brought smiles to everyone she met. Only a couple weeks after bringing her home, my father went into hospice; he had been battling cancer for several years. The facility allowed pets so ChiChi spent a week with me there visiting my dad. Although I had been preparing myself for losing him for a while, having her there with me made all the difference and helped me handle my dad's death emotionally.

ChiChi was one of the last things to bring a smile to his face, always sitting next to him on the bed and just laid her little head on his hand. His smile meant the world to me, and she got me through this painful period. Even though she was small, she was my rock and a big comfort. She brought smiles to many people that week; she was our little hero.

When we first got her, she was so tiny that she fit in my pocket. Eventually, she grew to be a whopping ten pounds of love, and although we only had her for a short time, she brought us so much joy and happiness. It was only a couple of months after we had her that she was spayed and micro-chipped. I felt terrible over the fact she went through surgery when she was so little. She was very attached to my husband and me. If she wasn't on my lap, then she was on my husband's chest giving him kisses. She was one of the cutest dogs ever, and she makes me want to believe there is something more out there, something after life, heaven perhaps? Losing her makes me "need" to know there is something else. Something higher than us, and that we will see her again, to hold her and tell her how sorry we are. That we were responsible for her death and that we should have been better at protecting her. It was a hard and valuable lesson.

CHICHI

My husband had never dealt with the death of a pet. Losing ChiChi was shocking to him, and I have never dealt with death well. I have found it even harder to deal with when it is a pet, maybe because they have been such a huge part of my everyday life. I have had many pets in my fifty years, many of them passing due to old age, but there were a few other tragic endings. Those were all hard and sad moments, but losing ChiChi hit me especially hard, as it should not have happened.

I am a firm advocate for adopting and I would absolutely adopt another dog. So many animals are euthanized every day. This is unnecessary and weighs heavily on my heart. I have never said no to taking in an animal in need. Whether I could keep them, or foster them until finding someone with more resources to give them a forever home.

We are grateful for our remaining five dogs; they all came to us at various times and in multiple ways. We love everything about our pets. They give me purpose and unconditional love. I can't imagine my life without pets.

If you are thinking about getting a pet, I will tell you they are not a disposable toy. You are all these animals have. You are in control of their happiness, sadness, safety, and entire well-being, providing daily for them as you would yourself with food, water, shelter and medical care. You need to be willing to sacrifice for them; they need to come first. It isn't fair to let them suffer. Be prepared and ready to provide them with your company and love! Remember to rescue or adopt, don't shop. It is selfish and irresponsible of humans to breed purposely for profit or to neglect spaying and neutering. Breeding for profit leads to far too many unwanted animals that deserve to live a good life but never get the chance.

More than likely, you will outlive your pet. Be prepared for that heartache, but then open your heart for another pet because there are so many animals that need us!

I hope that what I have shared can help someone else to be more responsible for the safety and well-being of their pets. I hope this helps prevent anyone else from going through what we went through.

It was very therapeutic getting this story down in writing even though it plays repeatedly in my head. I constantly imagine her being in that cold water, being trapped and terrified.

I considered going to a doctor for medical and psychological help. My depression was so severe I could hardly move. I missed more work than I could afford to. I'd been taking a prescription for this depression which has helped me cope much better. But not a day goes by I don't cry especially in the car when I am leaving or heading home. I'm worried about what else could happen to the other dogs, what I might find when I get back.

CHICHI

I hope that sharing my story it will help me find peace, and someday maybe I can forgive myself. My husband will also have to forgive himself.

ChiChi, we love you more than you could ever know.

Connie Niemeyer

Pets have taught me most of my life lessons.

To love unconditionally; to put others before me; the sense of responsibility; that I can't give up when others need me and the importance of relaxing and enjoying my time with them.

HEIDI

Iowa

1969 – 1980

HEIDI

She was a beautiful, reddish-brown color with big brown eyes, short hair, a long nose and body and short legs. Her name was Heidi.

My sisters, brothers and I didn't know we were getting a dog. Our parents mentioned nothing about it to us. I checked with my siblings to see what memories they had of Heidi.

My younger sister Kath told me, "I remember the day mom and dad went to go get her. I got off the bus from kindergarten, they locked the front door. I sat and cried on the front steps. They took longer than they thought to get her and get home before I did. I didn't know they were getting a dog."

My parents worked different shifts. My mom was a nurse at the hospital, and my dad was a radio dispatcher for the police department. So usually, there would be mom or dad at home sleeping during the day. All of us kids headed off to school, which left Heidi pretty much alone. What was a dog to do all day with no one to keep her company, or play with her except to find friends that would fill that void. We would come home from school and see her; she thought she was sneaky, hiding among all the stuffed animals she had dragged down to the living room. There were a lot of them she would pile on the sofa and then lay among them.

Sometimes after coming home from school or if we had gone somewhere for the entire day, we would find small bags of dog food shoved in between the cushions. Who knows why she put them there, maybe she thought if they don't come home soon or at all, I won't go hungry.

There were many times when Heidi got up on a kitchen chair or a dining room chair, and sat up like a little kid with her front paws on the edge of the table hoping someone would give her some bites. My brother Geno said he knew he could leave a plate of food on the floor while watching TV in the living room, go into the kitchen and come back, and she wouldn't touch it.

We loved going on vacations. About two weeks before school started in September is when we would go. Mom would get out the suitcases and tell us to get the clothes we wanted to wear, and she would pack. It never failed that Heidi would see that first suitcase come out, one minute you saw her, and next she disappeared. Heidi would get her leash that hung on a nail about five feet off the ground by the back door, and drag it down by the front door. Somehow she could always unhook it. Once everything was packed, suitcases were placed by the front door ready to be loaded into the station wagon. Heidi made sure that her bowls and pet rock were set at the front door as if to say "you are not leaving without me." She loved traveling with us.

A Dodge Maxivan was the next step up for our big family, trading in the old station wagon. There were six of us kids and Heidi. Many times we would find a KOA (Kamp of America) campground, where we also slept in the van. We each had our place at bedtime, either on a seat; across the front seats, alongside the door well or at the back of the van on top of all the suitcases and camping equipment. Heidi usually preferred sleeping with my sister Julie who was the petite one in the family. They slept on top of the luggage at the rear of the van. Mom and Dad slept on a make-shift bed on boards and foam across the top of the seats. Many times we felt like sardines in a can, but it was amazing to wake up among the clouds when we vacationed in the mountains.

We traveled to a lot of states. One of our vacations ended up being in January, and we headed down to Donna, Texas where our "snowbird" aunt and uncle lived during the winter months. It was so nice to be warm even if it was only for a week or so getting away from an Iowa winter. The Gulf of Mexico is where we all got our feet wet including Heidi. She had her pet rock and pushed it around in the wet sand with her nose. She'd bark at the waves and then go back to her rock. We didn't go anywhere without that rock.

My brother Dan remembers a time or two, which wasn't often, and on a family budget, that we would get a hotel room. Pets weren't allowed, so we had to sneak Heidi in under our coats, but she was always quiet.

Heidi got along well with just about everyone, with the usual barking first as a warning. After we calmed her down, and she could sniff whoever came to visit us, she was OK. She was quite protective of us kids. There was one time when Geno had friends over who knew we had a dog. They started wrestling and getting noisy. Heidi didn't like that at all and barked hoping that would deter the boys and make them stop. We told them to settle down or someone would get hurt as they were getting a little rough. One boy paid the price as

Heidi tried to take a bite out of his backside. That pretty well ended the rough play, and they never did it again.

Geno also remembers a few times when he would go shower down in the basement, on the concrete floor, that Heidi and her pet rock would visit him. She would shove her rock under the curtain and wait for him to push it back at her with his foot.

Feeding her table scraps, little by little she gained weight, and she looked more like a boloney dog instead of a wiener dog. We three older kids were off to college or working while the three younger ones were still at home going to school. I was living and working in Des Moines, Iowa and one evening I got a telephone call from my mom saying they had to put Heidi to sleep. She was getting older, and her eyesight was getting much worse, she was bumping into a lot of things. She had taken a bad fall down the basement stairs. All I remember mom saying was they had to put her to sleep and all I could say was "NO." I remember crying myself to sleep that night feeling so sad because I really missed Heidi, and I didn't have the chance to hold her or say goodbye.

Again, it was my younger sister Kath who remembered the day they put Heidi to sleep; Kath was sixteen. She had come home from school and Heidi was gone, kind of like the day she arrived, we didn't know, and we weren't told. Kath had gone to a basketball game that night as she was on the basketball team, and a teammate came into the locker room and asked her "what's the matter, you look like you lost your best friend," Kath wasn't good at hiding her emotions.

HEIDI

Having a pet, no matter what kind is a big responsibility. Animals cannot tell you what their needs are or what they are feeling. For anyone who is thinking about getting a pet, you need to weigh your pros and cons. Do your research to see what pet might fit you best and when you have decided, please take great care of them and love them, that's all they want. They will give you so much more in return, more than you could have imagined.

Trish Titus, Geno Grade, Kath Schroeder and Dan Grade

Heidi taught me responsibility and how to be more caring of others. I still miss her. – Trish

HERSHEY

Missouri

My husband, Ray, and his dog Hershey had a very special, intense, and loving bond. We had stopped at a Petco in Independence, Missouri to buy dog food for our other dogs Malachi (Great Dane) and Sophie (Italian Greyhound) when we noticed someone selling a litter of puppies for $50.00 each in the parking lot. He was the only chocolate Lab left, and he went home with us that day.

Ray and Hershey spent a lot of time together doing several activities including pheasant hunting, fishing, hiking, boating and snowball fights. Ray's father lived on some land in Pittsburg, Kansas that featured a twenty acre strip pit with a boathouse and dock. Every weekend we would load up the

Ray and Hershey - Big Air   *Speed Retrieve practice*

dogs and head for the country leaving the city in the rearview mirror. Hershey loved jumping off the dock or boat and splashing in the water, so Ray did some research and found a club called DockDogs.

DockDogs is a canine aquatics competition that humans and dogs can spend quality time together competing where the dogs jump off a dock into a pool filled with water. Hershey and Ray competed as a team in events titled Big Air (how far the dog jumps from the dock into the pool), Speed Retrieve (how quickly the dog retrieves a toy from the pool), Extreme Vertical (how high the dog jumps into the pool off the dock), and Iron Dog (dogs that compete in all three events).

Extreme Vertical practice

At 107 pounds, Hershey's personal bests were 21'6" Big Air; 7.332 Speed Retrieve, and 6'4" in Extreme Vertical. Anyone Ray ever met through DockDogs is because of Hershey.

Hershey at the FARGODOME, ND

They traveled all over the United States for competitions winning many ribbons and medals and making lifelong friends.

HERSHEY

Most of the competing dogs had DockDog trading cards they would exchange with each other during events and the yearend competition called Worlds.

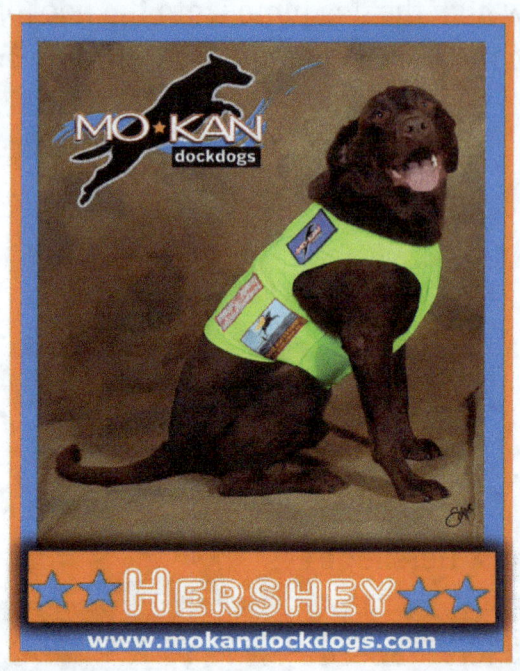

In 2010, Hershey was diagnosed with cancer. He went through two rounds of chemotherapy fighting like the brave, mighty dog he was, but after a short battle, unfortunately, he passed away in 2012 at the young age of six years old. He was surrounded in love by his family as he passed. We were utterly devastated, and for years our home felt empty and cold without his warm greetings, loving soul, huge smile and wet Hershey kisses.

Hershey was well known and loved by many people across the U.S. All his friends and fans felt his death.

The words following are taken from the Facebook video tribute my husband, Ray McCarty, created for Hershey:

12/11/12

"RIP my little buddy. He took his last breath about noon today in the presence of his family and his veterinarian. I'm glad he was able to spend some time with fellow DockDoggers from across the country this last weekend." –*Ray M.*

12/11/16

"Tomorrow at exactly 12:00 p.m. will be four years since Hershey's passing… I still get choked up at every single DockDogs event, although no one sees it, and probably three or four times a week. Despite what anyone says you never get over it; you learn to deal with the pain and loneliness. He had probably fifty different handlers or more take part with him on the dock from the east to the west coast. Hershey happily taught new handlers how to do big air, speed retrieve, and extreme vertical moves. If someone new showed up with a dog that didn't want to take part, he was glad to step in and let the handler have a good time."–*Ray M.*

"RIP Hershey man."

Amber & Ray McCarty

HERSHEY

Ray saw this brochure at a DockDogs event he attended. It was a photo he had taken of Hershey getting a treatment.

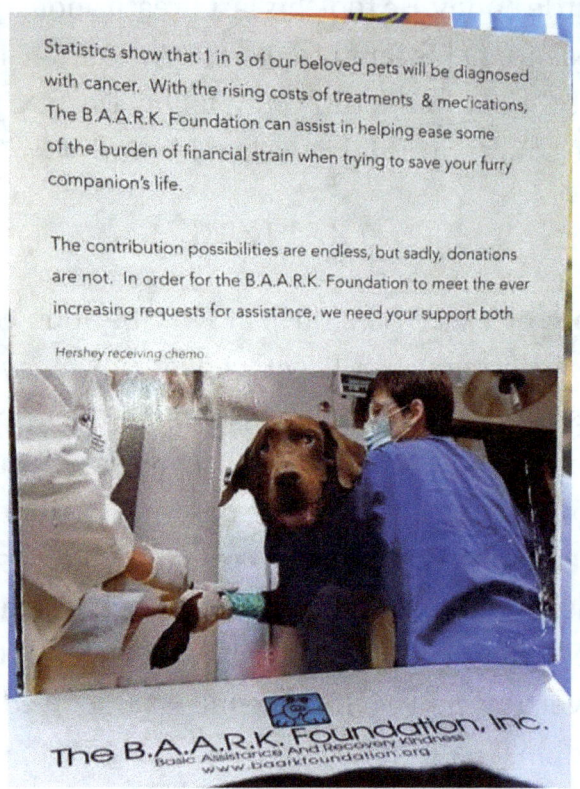

One of Hershey's Chemotherapy sessions, a very courageous boy.

If you would like to learn more about the B.A.A.R.K Foundation, Inc., and how you can help, check out their website (permission granted to use brochure cover) at www.baarkfoundation.org

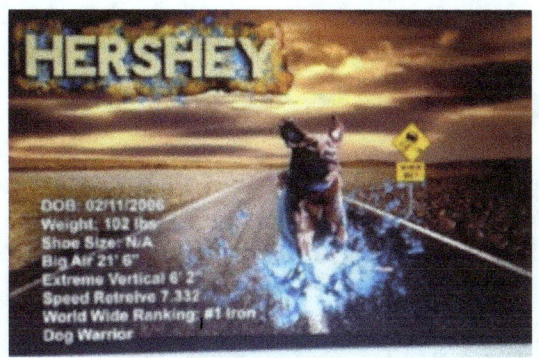

Miss you Hershey!

TANJIE CAT MILLER

Missouri

1994 – 2015

TANJIE CAT MILLER

Licking fingers or the chin,
Is the greeting to her people kin.
A very oral cat, loving kisses she gives,
Kneading a soft blanket, her kittenhood relives.
Each morning I would lift the shade,
As by the window on a pillow, Tanjie laid.
Curled with her paw over her eyes to shield the light,
Such a golden orange striped coat,
and yellow eyes so bright.
Climbing the backyard tree and rolling in the sun,
Jumping the fence, she'd come to the front door when done.
With a meow, she'd carry a string to me for us to play,
Then nap under the comforter during the mid-day.
Once a very strong cat, she did chin-ups on the
scratching post, and played swat the ball
of long hits, she could boast.
As a young kitty, she was an intelligent, feisty brat,
Knocking over vases and cups, a curious cat;
To tell me she was sick, upset or ornery,
On the carpet, she would pee.
Seven years older, sister hated to be chased,
But would play with paws through the two-seater space.
After sister died, Tanjie's temperament changed,
A quieter disposition emerged, more tamed.
She even developed much softer fur,
And more frequently had a marvelous purr.
A more friendly and affectionate girl,
Jumping on my keyboard for attention she'd curl.

Seven years younger, brother often wanted to play,
Even if Tanjie would try to hiss him away.
Tanjie would shake paws with me when she was fed,
And at night, would curl on my feet on my bed.
Turkey baby food, shrimp, and milk she adored,
She'd nudge brother away so she could get more.
Begging for deli turkey, she takes from my fingers,
With front feet on the cabinet door, she lingers.
I'll miss the most this ritual delight,
As my pretty Tanjie kitty fades from my sight.
More than nine lives my "sweet pie" used
in the last seven years,
But her loss breaks my heart, laden with my tears.

Tanjie's poem by Carol Miller

March 27, 2008, edited July 4, 2015, after her death

LADDIE
Minnesota/Wisconsin

1999 – 2012

LADDIE

Collies have always been my favorite dogs. I imagine it has something to do with watching Lassie on TV growing up, but to me, they are the most beautiful dogs. Their loving and friendly nature makes me think they are the perfect family dog.

After the death of our previous dog, Ollie the Collie, we explored finding another dog through a rescue group. It felt right to look for a dog that had already been abandoned or disadvantaged. It was like rooting for the underdog!

We saw a photo of Laddie on the Minnesota Wisconsin Collie Rescue website and wrote to ask if we could foster him. After getting the go-ahead, we drove five hours from Wauwatosa, (a suburb of Milwaukee) Wisconsin to St. Paul, Minnesota to pick him up. When we arrived at the home where he was staying, we rang the doorbell. The homeowner didn't appear, but a beautiful sable Collie did, and he stood at the door, quietly eyeing us up. I think we knew even then that he would be a "foster failure" or a dog that comes for the short term fostering and never leaves.

Laddie spent the first five years of his life caged in a dog run in someone's backyard. He had little interaction or exercise, and one of his neighbors saw this and felt sorry for him. She commented to his owners about how beautiful he was. Their response was, "Do you want him?" She took him into her home and then contacted the rescue group.

Lad was the most loving dog. He was so affectionate and loved to snuggle next to me on the couch. If I was reading on the bed, he would jump up next to me, lay down with a moan and throw a leg over me. If I didn't scratch him, he would tap at me with his paw, as if to say "hey, I'm here. Why are you not loving me up?"

When we adopted Lad, we had three cats. Our orange tabby, Cisco, the elder statesman of our cats, gave him an orientation as to who was in charge on his first day in the house. Lad sauntered up to him for a smell, and the cat reared up on his hind legs and gave Lad's muzzle a sound boxing. Lad understood this lesson, and there was never any conflict between them. They spent many winter days snuggled up together for warmth.

Laddie – summer run

He lived for long walks and off-leash running in the park near our home. He would run like the wind, and my husband took many beautiful photos of him, running at high speed. We called some of these fantastic pictures his supermodel shots. He was a gentle companion to our four children. We have many memories of his goofy behavior.

Laddie – winter run

No counter was safe from Lad. He would stand on his hind legs, and with his long Collie snout, he could reach even the farthest corners of the countertops. We put any food that didn't need refrigerated in the microwave over the stove, which to this day is referred to as "the dog box."

One day I opened the refrigerator, and a rotisserie chicken fell out. The lid flew off, and in a blink Lad had the whole bird in his mouth and took off running. Knowing that cooked chicken bones are dangerous for dogs, I was yelling at him to drop it, but he ran through the house trying to find a safe corner to consume the spoils. He was trying to chew as he ran, but his mouth was open so wide to hold the chicken that he could only make growling sounds. I finally cornered him near a doorway and have vivid memories of pulling chicken parts out both sides of his mouth while he tried to ingest it. My daughter remembers that he grabbed a loaf of bread one time and took off with it.

I also remember that he used to sit under the table when we were eating. When he smelled something he liked, he would sneak his muzzle up over the edge of the table quickly to try and snag a treat. We called it his "stealth muzzle."

Laddie loved to ride in the car. We took him up north to stay at a friend's cabin on Rock Lake as well as a state park in Northern Wisconsin. But mainly our trips took us to visiting family in Iowa.

LADDIE

He loved riding on our pontoon boat and would sit in the very front like the captain, with his fur blowing in the wind. However, he would NOT, under any circumstance enter the water, not even to get his feet wet.

Blue on the left, Laddie on the right

When Lad was around thirteen, he started to have (GI) Gastrointestinal issues. We pursued different treatments, but nothing seemed to treat the problems. He still loved his walks, ate well, and was his usual affectionate self.

One morning I let him out into the yard, and when I came back, he was calmly sitting, but wouldn't get up, not even for a treat. When I tried to coax him into the house, he wouldn't move. So we scooped him up and headed to our vet. We called our children on the way so they could meet us there. The doctor felt that Lad was bleeding internally and given his condition and age, we chose not to pursue any diagnostic tests (x-rays, etc.) or any other treatments.

We made the difficult decision needed for this beautiful dog of ours. Several of the kids could be there until the end. It was incredibly sad, to have had the unconditional love of this amazing dog for so many years, was a gift. We all told him how much we loved him, what a good dog he was and how much we would miss him, while we stroked his fur and scratched all his favorite spots.

Laddie was the best dog I've ever had. Our children are grown and out on their own; we're hesitant to have another dog. We also wonder if any other dog would be a disappointment after having such a special one.

Lori Grade

Lad helped me learn to slow down, take time for a walk, a scratch and a snuggle. He knew that the best part of life was being with your people.

MOZART
Minnesota

September 1987 - November 2, 2001

MOZART

I had never had a close relationship with a dog until Mozart. My daughter, Heidi, was seventeen and decided that she'd never had a pet of her own, so one Saturday we drove up to Circle of Friends Humane Society in Grand Forks, North Dakota. We lived across the Red River in East Grand Forks, Minnesota. Circle of Friends was the only Humane Society in the area. Heidi picked up this eight-week-old puppy that someone had adopted and returned. She carried him around until we had to leave. Circle of Friends was closing until the following Tuesday; we decided that Mozart would be our dog, so we filled out the paperwork and paid the $25.00 fee. They told us we could get a refund if we had him neutered and vaccinated, so we did.

We nicknamed him Motzi. Motzi was a cross between a Springer Spaniel and a black Lab. He was all black with a bit of white under his chin. His tail was long and curled up.

He chewed up several pairs of my most expensive shoes and escaped from the kennel we made for him in the basement. I let him sleep near me at night so I could tell when he needed to go outside.

In 1994, we moved to Pickerel Lake, Minnesota. Motzi loved it there and could go out whenever he wanted. He never left the yard without a family member. He was quite the swimmer and would run off the end of the dock to dive before swimming back to shore. He loved riding in the car traveling with us almost everywhere and was a great walking companion.

It was nine years later (1996) that we adopted a cat named Rescue. Rescue belonged to my son, Scott, and he gave him to us when he and his family moved into their new home. Whenever my husband and I went for our walks, Motzi would lead the parade with Rescue trailing along behind him.

When my husband and I split up, Rescue went to live with Heidi who was living on her own and Motzi moved with me to an apartment in Battle Lake, Minnesota. He developed problems with his back legs and had to have three surgeries. He wasn't doing well at all. On November 29, 2001, I made the difficult decision to have Motz put to sleep, he was thirteen years old. I held him in my arms; it was such a sad day for me. He had such a wonderful and unique personality, and he brought such joy to me. Motzi turned out to be the best friend one could ever have.

Marcia Olson

Motzi taught me about loyalty and to have fun.
He taught me to take time and enjoy life,
because it can all be gone without notice.

JEFÉ
Iowa

May 2015 – January 11, 2017

JEFÉ

Telephone interview with Shawn about Jefé

Trish: I emailed you originally to see if you could provide me with some information on how to contact one of your horse boarders, as I had learned the horse had died. This horse had been a lesson horse for a long time at your stable. My daughter had taken riding lessons on this particular horse and I was hoping that the owner might be willing to share his story and memories. You told me you would pass my email along to him.

I then asked if you knew of anyone who had lost a pet and would be open and willing to share their memories. You replied that you wanted to share your story about your pet goat.

Can you tell me his name?

Shawn: His name was Jefé. J-E-F-É.

Trish: Tell me again.

Shawn: Jefé, it sounds like the J is an H. (Hef-ay)

Trish: That's different. How did you acquire him?

Shawn: Jefé was given to me by my fiancée; it was our anniversary in June of 2015. Jefé was four weeks old, and she surprised me with him. I have pictures from the very first thirty minutes I held him, up until the day he died. So, he was an anniversary gift.

Trish: Did you always want a goat or was that kind of a surprise to you?

Shawn: I don't know why, but for some reason, ever since I was a kid I was in love with goats. Elizabeth and I talked about it many times. I thought they were a cool animal. Goats were something that I always wanted. I've never owned goats growing up, and I didn't know anything about them. I just thought they were a cool animal. It was a learning process when I first got him. I knew from a very young age that I always wanted two goats and I wanted to name them Jefé and Rico.

Trish: Jefé and Rico, those are different names.

Shawn: When I got him, I said OK, I already knew what I wanted his name to be.

Trish: You mentioned to me that he was a Nigerian Dwarf?

Shawn: Right, he was a Nigerian Dwarf.

Trish Are those common here in the United States?

Shawn: Yes, they are quite common. Goats are primarily raised for dairy and showing. The goats don't get very big, and they aren't necessarily used for meat. But, their milk has the highest fat content of any other goat. They are used a lot for goat based soaps, lotions, and things like that.

Trish: I didn't know that. So when you got Jefé, was he from Iowa or from somewhere else?

Shawn: Elizabeth got him from a lady here in Iowa.

Trish: Are there quite a few goat farmers all over?

Shawn: There are tons of breeders in Iowa. They are a prevalent 4-H type showing goat.

Trish: Tell me how you came up with his name again?

Shawn: I'm not sure. I think because of my dad. He was in the military, and he did a lot of work in South America. I think I remember him telling a story which included people named Rico and Jefé and I believe that those two names just kind of stuck with me. It could have been from my childhood or related to my father. I remember that Jefé was a cool sounding name.

Trish: Did Jefé do any traveling with you?

Shawn: No, we never did any traveling with Jefé. However, he loved to ride with us up to the Kum and Go gas station which is near the barn as well as short rides to places in town, but he would stay in the car.

Trish: I would imagine that you had a lot of people staring at you as you're going down the road? (Laughs)

Shawn: Yes, I've had people come up to the window and ask "is that a goat?" (Chuckles)

Trish: So what were some fun and silly things that you remember about Jefé? Did he hang around with the other animals on the property?

Shawn: We have a calico barn cat, and her name is Myra. Myra is a mean cat. She won't let you pet her anywhere past her head; she doesn't like being held or cuddled. She's just an ornery cat, but Jefé and Myra for some reason formed the most amazing bond. Anytime we let Jefé go outside when the weather was pleasant, he would wander around and be grazing and no matter where he went, Myra was always with him. You never saw Jefé outside without Myra somewhere nearby. Jefé was an inside goat. He was potty trained. He slept in the bed with us, sat on the couch and watched TV with us; he was like a dog. He did a lot of things with us.

Jefé got along well with our big Labrador, Zeus, and our little miniature Doberman Pinscher, Hera, actually all the other animals. He just fit right in. We always said we didn't think he knew that he was a goat. We had pet rats, and he would let them come around him when he was lying on the couch, but their little whiskers would tickle his legs, and Jefé would jump up, he was so funny. (Chuckles)

Trish: How was Jefé with other humans?

Shawn: For whatever reason, Jefé loved children. He would be in the barn and hear a kid (child) come in, and he would run to find them. When young students would come out to the stable to take their riding lessons, he would run towards them, and they all just wanted to play. It got to where the kids were more excited to see Jefé than they were to be in a horse barn for their lesson.

All the horse boarders dearly loved him. They would set their tack and grooming equipment down, and he would rub them to see if they had any treats. They would always bring peppermints to the horses, and they'd bring peppermints for Jefé. He loved the attention.

Trish: You mentioned that Jefé was your shadow from the time he was four weeks old until his death at a year and eight months old. Tell me about that.

Jefé in his little horse blanket he wore in winter.

Shawn: Yes, he was born in May 2015 and died January 11, 2017. Several days or so before taking him to the vet is when we noticed his behavior changing, his appetite had decreased, and he wasn't producing normal urine output. We brought him to the vet at 11:00 p.m. on January 10th, he stayed overnight, and they ran tests. Jefé was diagnosed with Urinary Calculi. It's a protein imbalance in their body which makes it hard for them to relieve themselves (this is very common in castrated or "wethered" goats) and it develops typically in older goats, anywhere from one or two years of age up to five or six years of age.

We had our suspicions about his diagnosis before we took him in and then after the tests, the veterinarian confirmed that it was Urinary Calculi. Typically, it's a fatal diagnosis, and if they do perform surgery, it's on a meat goat that they are just trying to put enough weight on to go to market. It's not a good solution for a pet, as a blockage will recur; or they won't have control over their bladder; and it's excruciating. They think this happened to Jefé because he was wethered so young at four weeks old. His anatomy didn't have time to develop all the way as it should have before being wethered by the breeder.

When Jefé was diagnosed with this problem, the vet gave us some surgical options; however, they were very costly ($2,000.00 and up and would have been very painful), and the surgery is a temporary fix until goats go to slaughter. It's not a permanent fix for a pet. Jefé was already in pain.

By 10:00 a.m. the next morning, January 11th, we made the heartbreaking decision to put him down. I brought him home that morning, and I spent the entire day with him, just loving him and holding him. We watched TV and ate snacks like we always did. The vet came out that evening as we sat on the couch, Jefé lay on my lap with his head on my right arm, and the vet came in and gave him the sedative and then the medication to put him to sleep while I was holding him. It was 5:48 p.m. when he died. It was nice that he didn't know what was going on, but it was gut-wrenching for me, and I felt like I couldn't breathe. It was so difficult to let him go because I loved him so much. It happened so fast. He was in pain, and we couldn't allow that to happen any longer. I now just sat there and held onto him a bit longer.

He imprinted on me because he was so young when I got him. Jefé followed me everywhere I went. If I was on the small tractor, he followed the tractor. The same with the 4-wheeler when I was unloading hay. Sometimes he rode on the hay wagon with me. When he had gotten a little older, he would stay outside to graze. He could recognize our car coming up the driveway and came running because he knew we were home. Jefé was very smart, and he knew us very well and just loved being around us, and to me, that was the hardest part. I had this shadow for more than a year and a half and then all of a sudden he was gone. It was truly difficult for me. I was more attached to him then I had been to any other pet. As the barn manager, I'm always at the barn. Jefé was always there with me, and that's what made losing him so very difficult, this awesome companion who was always there, now gone.

Our vet bill exceeded $500.00. A couple of days after his passing, I wasn't sure how we were going to pay for it. Our veterinarian, Dr. Howard, the receptionist and all the boarders at the barn paid Jefé's bill off entirely. That's how well everyone liked him. It was amazing. It was very touching and very emotional. We realized that as much as we loved him, everyone else loved him too.

Trish: It is a big responsibility to take care of them, they need us, and we need them. When they die, sometimes it seems to be more than we can handle.

Shawn: When Jefé died, Myra would come into the house every single night looking for him. She'd go to the couch; she'd go to his kennel and our bedroom looking for him. She would wander around the house for about thirty minutes meowing at the top of her lungs, a yell that we had never heard from her before just looking for him. Finally, Myra would come in and settle down on the couch and rest. But every single night for at least a month after he died she came in looking for him.

Trish: She really missed him. There are people who don't think animals have feelings, yet they create these beautiful bonds with other animals outside their own species, and those connections are so strong.

Shawn: Yes, they were absolutely the best of friends. Even though he had little nubs instead of horns, she was the only cat he wouldn't throw them (toss his head) at as well as the only cat Jefé wouldn't head-butt, and she was the only one that could stand near him while he was eating. He wouldn't let the dogs stand next to him or anybody else, he didn't want anybody near him while he was eating. Myra was the only one. And Myra, the only animal that she would rub up against was Jefé; she wouldn't rub up against any other animal. It was difficult for her when he died; she was very heartbroken.

JEFÉ

With Jefé, I think the weirdest thing with him is that it's not a bond you expect to form with an animal like that. You go into it owning an animal like a goat thinking of them as a simple farm animal, but there was something different about Jefé. He was very capable of giving and receiving love. He was a very affectionate goat. People don't often see that side of them. I'm a practical person. I have friends that slaughter goats and stuff like that. I know the bond between Jefé and I was an atypical (unusual) relationship. He was a different kind of animal that I never expected to have as a pet, and I created such a bond with him.

Trish: You had mentioned that your mother passed away some months before Jefé did.

Shawn: July of 2016, six months before Jefé died, I lost my mother unexpectedly. My father passed thirteen years ago, and now I needed to go home for a week to bury my mom and get her estate settled. Elizabeth and everybody at the barn said Jefé had dropped weight because he wouldn't eat and he consistently called for me. He loved Elizabeth very much, they were great together, and she loved him as well. But he went through a depression when I left, and that took Jefé on a downhill slide. It was too much for him to recuperate. He got so depressed and then having this health issue.

My mom had been ill for quite some time; she was elderly and was not doing well at all. I think she was ready to be with my dad. She'd been in the hospital but died at home; she'd lived a good life. As hard as it is to say, losing Jefé was worse than losing my mother. It was different because he couldn't help what happened to him, he was so young and full of life. I had such a connection with Jefé that losing him felt like I lost a person in my life that fit a specific need that only he could give to me.

Trish: I'm sorry about both of them. Would you consider another pet?

Shawn: About two weeks after Jefé died I told Elizabeth I wanted another goat, but I just wasn't sure when I would be ready. I feared that I would draw comparisons between a new pet and the old one. I would have to remind myself that there will never be another goat like Jefé. How could I live with and have that kind of relationship with another goat? I knew after being away from Jefé for just a few weeks, it was the funny little things they do and the way they are that helped us to decide. Very quickly I realized I enjoyed that relationship so much and I wanted to give more, so we started looking and found a breeder.

When we decided to get another goat, we decided that we would get two girls because girls almost never have the urinary problems that wethered goats do.

I'll have to tell you, Jefé, had his voice like all of our animals have their voice. I would always talk in a little voice for Jefé, and we would talk to Elizabeth and the other animals in the house. Jefé told a story about an Aunt Rosa, and he would say "Let me tell you about the time that my Aunt Rosa..." and then he would tell the story. Even though it was a story, our first little girl was named Rosa, after Jefé's "Aunt Rosa." We got Rosa when she was twenty-four hours old. We would name the other one "Hilly," which is my mom's maiden name Hill. Elizabeth says all the time, I don't believe in reincarnation, but if I did, I could swear that Jefé was inside of Rosa. When we brought her home and the very first night we got into bed, not only did she get up into the bed and was comfortable, but she went to the same spot that Jefé would usually sleep in and the same position.

She was potty trained within a week. She wasn't afraid of our dogs or other pets. It's like she knew where everything was, she knew how to be in the house and out on the farm. Jefé always had a healthy fear of horses, Rosa doesn't, and she is fearless; so we are training her to have a healthy fear of horses as well as the 4-wheeler and other vehicles. She's still learning, but it's almost like having Jefé around.

We are waiting for the second baby to be born so Rosa will have a friend. We want a girl; we just can't get another boy because they are so prone to that blockage. I don't know that I can go through losing another goat like that. I didn't expect to have Jefé for only a year a half, that's what was difficult.

Trish: His passing was too soon.

Shawn: I'm a better person for having known Jefé.

Trish: I think that's what they do, they make us better. What do you think Jefé has taught you?

Shawn: I'm a woman with a woman. That makes me a little different than most people in the world, but the other thing is that I'm not afraid to do things differently. With Jefé, it's just reminded me that love doesn't always come in pretty little boxes or the same packaging that everybody else sees. Love comes in many different forms. It's not what you typically think of in your life with how and where you receive love and respect. And I think if more people would just open themselves up to accepting any affection or any love across the board, the world would be in a much better place, no matter what you look like on the exterior that love can come from anything. And most often it comes from the least expected things.

Trish: Unconditional love.

Shawn: And loyalty. Jefé, the minute I was loyal to him, he was loyal to me, and that was the bond that we had. I didn't see him differently than anything else, and I don't think he saw me any differently than anything else. Elizabeth always said that she doesn't know if Jefé felt that he was a human or that he thought that I was a goat.

Trish: Thank you, Shawn.

Jefé and Shawn

BUDDY & DANTE

Missouri

Buddy with owner Janie

May 1999 – August 2014

At one time, my husband and I had five large dogs, all living in our home. This is the story of Buddy and Dante, the first dogs in our family.

My eighteen-year-old daughter brought this cute little black fur ball home late one night with a "story," that he was going to be taken out in the country and dropped off by some kids she knew, to fend for himself if she did not take him. The puppy looked like a miniature black Lab with Terrier ears and could almost fit in the palms of our hands. We let our daughter keep this adorable little black fur ball. After two weeks, my daughter moved out and went to live with her father, but Buddy, who I named, stayed. Buddy went everywhere with us. If we went for ice cream, he came along. If we went to the lake for the weekend, he went.

DANTE
August 2001 – October 2011

Dante with our grandkids

About a year later, my son, who was living with his father, brought Dante to our house for the weekend. My son got Dante from a teacher at his school, and it was my son that named him. Dante was part Brittney and part Siberian Husky. He had the most beautiful coat that went from dark chestnut brown to pure white on the tips of his tail, paws and belly. About a month later while with my son at his father's house, Dante developed an ear problem and came to live with us for treatment; guess what, he never left.

Dante tried everything to get Buddy to play with him. He would drag Buddy out of the house by his collar trying to get him to play. Dante was much bigger and stronger than Buddy, but Buddy was stubborn and refused to play with Dante. Buddy would rather play with his human family.

Buddy and Dante didn't know they were dogs because they were never really treated like dogs. We talked to them and took them everywhere with us. Both of them loved the water, and when we were at the lake, we would take them out on the pontoon boat to a small island to let them run and play. We would dock the boat on the island, and they would jump off so excited and head straight for the water to swim.

You can't imagine the looks and stares we received when people would see Buddy and Dante riding the jet skis with my husband and me, or Buddy tubing with me behind the boat. As I said, neither of them seemed to realize they were dogs.

Dante didn't have a mean bone in his body. He was happy all the time, but his favorite time was when the grandkids came to visit. From the time they were babies, Dante loved being around them. The more they pulled on his tail and lay on top of him, the happier he was. If we took Dante anywhere, he headed straight for a group of kids. Dante was a rather large dog. Some of the kids were afraid of him at first; but he won the kids over because he was so loveable and just wanted to play with them.

When Dante was about ten years old, we noticed that he was losing weight and not eating well. We took him to our veterinarian and after surgery we were told that Dante had cancer. We then took him to a cancer specialist in Kansas City and were told that they could do a second surgery and chemotherapy, but it would only extend his life by three to six months. We were told that if we did nothing, he would only survive two to three months. We didn't want to prolong his suffering, so we decided to forego the surgery and chemotherapy and make his last days as wonderful as possible. About a week later, my husband took off work for a few days and took Dante to his favorite place, the lake house.

I received a call two days later informing me that if I wanted to see Dante, I needed to come that day. There were only ten days between the time he was diagnosed and the time we had to have him put to sleep. I never knew that I could be so heartbroken over the loss of a pet. I'd never had a pet before and did not understand at first that they become part of the family. Even to this day, there are times I still get teary-eyed when thinking about him.

About three months after Dante died, Buddy, age twelve, would not eat; he was having difficulty breathing, and could barely stand. So, on a Saturday morning, my husband and I took him to the vet where he ran some tests and then came out and told us that he had bad news. After losing Dante, we feared the worst. We learned that Buddy had diabetes and we were actually relieved and could breathe a little easier. I didn't know that dogs could get diabetes. Normal sugar levels for dogs are the same as they are for humans (around 100). Buddy's sugar level was so high that their machine couldn't even register it. Buddy would have to stay the night. The following day, Sunday, we got a call and were told that his sugar levels had dropped…they were now at 650, but Buddy still would not eat. Our vet didn't know if Buddy could survive if he didn't begin eating soon. For a week, my husband and I each made daily trips to hand feed Buddy. About a week later, Buddy was able to come home.

Once he was home, we had to give him insulin shots twice a day for his sugar. Then, every three months he needed to spend the day at the vet's office so they could monitor his sugar levels and adjust his insulin. For more than two years, we followed this same routine. When Buddies breathing problems returned, we took him back to our vet and more tests run. Our vet told us that Buddy had a large tumor pressing on his lungs as well as other tumors throughout his body. A week or so later, we had to have Buddy put to sleep.

BUDDY & DANTE

Buddy and Dante are both buried next to each other at our house at the lake. They both loved the water and being at the lake, and that is where they will remain forever.

Now my husband and I only have three dogs: Bonnie, Clyde and Ranger. Bonnie and Clyde are fifteen-year-old brother and sister, solid white Shepherd, and Husky mixes. Ranger is a black and white Husky who is seven years old. We acquired these three when they were quite young and they found their forever home with us.

My husband worked nights and I worked days. When the kids got older and moved out on their own, the dogs were our company. We would talk to them and not feel so alone. I know we have some tough times ahead as Bonnie and Clyde are getting older, but I would do it again in a heartbeat.

Janie Williams

My dogs taught me that pets are comforting and make life happier. If you are having a bad day, they make you feel better. If you are lonely, they make you feel not so alone. They are always glad to see you and are always there for you.

PRINCE

Iowa

After playing in the dirt it was time for a bath.

1981 ~ 1992

PRINCE

It was 1981. Prince was just a couple months old, and even though Deb and I had only been together for a couple months, she picked him out just for me. Her best friend's dad raised purebred Collies, and she was able to get one from them. He was so white, which was rare, most are not that color. Prince had sable coloring in his collar and mane, and a brown spot above his tail. We named him Prince after his dad.

After Deb and I got married, we lived in one or two places that weren't too far from our original hometowns. In the fall of 1987, my parents bought an acreage about seven miles from where they lived. They planned to raise llamas so they could sell the wool, use them as pack animals and show them at county and state fairs. They needed someone to help manage the llamas and someone they could trust; it was then that Deb and I moved onto the acreage. All this space gave Prince lots of room to roam and grow. He also kept many unwelcomed critters at bay. Prince enjoyed running the fence line barking at the llamas as did the other dogs that eventually came into our lives after Prince's passing.

I was home and happened to be outside one day when I heard a commotion and went to see what it was. Prince had gotten into the llama pen and the llamas had him cornered and pinned down (they are excellent guard animals). He was a good-sized collie, but they wouldn't let him up, so I knew I had to go into the pen and physically pick him up and carry him out. Except for those llamas, he was very friendly and got along well with everyone. He was great with our daughters as they were growing up.

Prince was no exception when it came to thunderstorms. If we knew a storm was coming, we let him inside. Most dogs don't like storms, and if they are outside, they will run at the first opportunity trying to get away from the sound of thunder and lightning. One severe storm popped up, and he took off, we found him a day later at the airport which was about four miles away. And then several years later another severe storm scared him, and he took off running, ultimately he ended up getting hit by a vehicle on the highway right south of our home in front of the cemetery. That was in 1992. That was a horrible, sad day. Prince was a wonderful pet, and like all of our pets, we miss him very much. As hard as we might try, we will never be able to replace him.

For anyone thinking about getting a pet, there are many things to consider: will they be a companion for you or your children, do you enjoy taking off on weekends or longer and have your pet accompany you or will you have to leave them at home with someone who can care for them.

You'll want to do some research regarding the details about the breed, purebred or otherwise. Find out what the animal may be prone to having medically like seizures, hip problems, diabetes, and so on. Sometimes there are things you can do for them to help prolong their life and sometimes there may not be much you can do for them except to let them go.

Geno Grade

WINNIE
Wisconsin

Matt with a sleeping Winnie

Unknown ~ 2013

WINNIE

My husband, Matt, and I adopted Winnie in the summer of 2012, shortly after we got married. We wanted our dog, Zoe, to have a companion while we were both away at work, so we decided to start looking around. We went to the Wisconsin Humane Society in Milwaukee, and it was there that they had a whole suite called the Cat Palace which was broken down into smaller rooms. Each room held no more than two or three cats. At the end of the row, there was a room that was about seven feet long and four feet wide, and one whole side of this room was a window. There were two cats in this room; one perched on a cat tree which was right up against the window and the other had one paw on the glass door into this room.

When I put my hand on the door on the opposite side of the glass from her, she started pawing at the glass as if she was trying to get closer to me. We found a staff employee right away because we wanted to put a hold on her so that no one else could adopt her until we met her. Fudgie, the name given to her by the Humane Society was a beautiful, small, domestic short-haired cat, almost brindled (a coat coloring pattern, described as "tiger-striped") brown and gray.

When we were allowed into her small glass room, she immediately jumped into my lap and started rubbing her head against my face, and she stole my heart. Even though she was small, she was a very interactive cat and the most lovable girl we found. We decided right then that we wanted to adopt her. We filled out the necessary paperwork and she came home with us that day. Her incredibly cuddly nature reminded me of a teddy bear, so the only fitting name was my old childhood favorite Winnie from "Winnie the Pooh."

Winnie loved to emulate Winnie's friend Tigger and pounce. You could play a game of fetch with her. We had a small cat toy shaped like a bright pink mouse that I would throw to the other side of the room. Winnie would dart after it, pounce on it and bring it back to me proudly dropping her (pretend) kill into my lap. I would throw it again, and she would once more return to me with her prize. We could play this game for an hour. Winnie also loved playing with balls, feathers, and yarn, almost anything that moved.

She not only enjoyed pouncing on toys but also on people's heads. My friend, Liz, was visiting one day, and Winnie seemed very fascinated with Liz's long hair. In a matter of minutes, Winnie had jumped and landed, sprawled out, claws scrambling to try and find a hold on my friend's poor head. I still can't quite figure out how she managed to stay up on Liz's head, even for the few seconds that she managed to hang on before being forcibly removed.

Winnie not only loved to curl up and cuddle with humans, but you could also find her snuggled up on our bed with her other furry companions, Zoe, our Shih Tzu, and Alvin, who was our next adopted friend, an enormous, fluffy, Tabby cat. Alvin didn't always appreciate cuddles so occasionally they would have a little boxing match.

Winnie absolutely loved humans. So much so to the point that if you ignored her, she would bite your book, sit on your phone, your computer and even your face to force you to pay attention to her. I have quite the number of books with either torn off corners or where you can still see the teeth marks.

Sometimes she would drape herself on your shoulder for a nap like a baby. My husband, Matt, tried to teach her to jump on his shoulders. After receiving several large scratches from her back claws, the jumping lessons ended quickly.

Winnie loved to curl up on your lap as well as spread herself out and almost always wore a smirk on her face.

When we adopted Winnie, the Humane Society thought that she was at least one year old, but didn't have a definite age. Not knowing her age made it even harder when she started getting sick just one year later. Our best estimation, she couldn't have been more than three or four the summer of 2013.

Winnie started getting pretty sick. She had begun to scoot across the floor the way many pets do, and then we noticed blood in her urine. We took her to the vet, and he said that he needed to get a sterile urine sample to culture so he could figure out what was going on. To do this with a cat, you need to insert a needle through the abdomen, into the bladder while it is full to retrieve enough urine. Our vet said the best way to get a cat to hold their urine, to get the sample, is to keep them in a cage without a litterbox. So the plan was for her to spend the night and I would pick her up after I got off work the next day. Three days later she was still there, with every attempt the same, to get a urine sample. As soon as our vet would come near her with the needle, she would immediately pee. After those three days, our vet said that it was too much stress for her, and he would just put her on a broad-spectrum antibiotic that would hopefully take care of whatever bacteria were causing the issue. Well, that plan didn't work. She kept getting worse, and her urine kept getting darker and darker.

Throughout this, like any animal, Winnie was acting a lot less energetic than usual. She was usually a bounce off the walls kind of cat, and she was sleeping more. It was hard to tell how much she was eating and drinking since we had two cats at the time who shared the same bowls.

Our next options after the broad spectrum antibiotics were probably sending her to an animal hospital to see if they could get the sample that our vet couldn't, but we simply didn't have the funds. There were no other medication options available within our budget. And since we didn't know what exactly was causing her to be so sick, and the intensive care to try and get more answers was going to be way too expensive.

It finally got to the point where our vet said that her quality of life was so low that it wasn't worth trying another medication. It was the hardest decision in the world to let her go. To this day the only information that we had is that she had some type of bladder infection (hence the blood in her urine) which could have been the primary culprit or a result of something else.

Since Winnie's passing, we haven't gotten another cat. Maybe one day as our kids get older we will find another special kitty. I wish my children had the chance to meet Winnie. I would love for my kids to have the experience of growing up with an awesome pet. Her personality was amazing. She was the sweetest, most cuddly cat ever.

I don't regret adopting her one bit, but I do regret that we didn't catch her being sick earlier so that she could have been treated sooner. Winnie died too young; she was an amazing and loving cat.

Hannah Hubert

The most important lesson she taught me is that life is fleeting, especially those of our furry friends. Enjoy every minute and take advantage of the time you have.

TOOTSIE

Missouri

1988 – 2003

TOOTSIE

Many moons ago a friend of mine, who is also an animal rescuer, called and said she had received information about a small dog, believed to be a Yorkie, which was found roaming the streets. We hit the road to rescue this baby with high hopes of finding it a "furever" home, thinking it would be darn easy to rehome a Yorkie (*well, the joke was on us*).

When we arrived, there were three medium sized dogs and a small, gray, elderly mutt dog, so obviously not a Yorkie. The dog could barely walk, and it didn't even cross my mind that this was the dog she had called about, but of course, it was. I gathered up the little old lady and got back in the car certain that we would never find this poor dog a home.

After we got home, I gave her a bath and got her acclimated to my dogs. That evening, I realized this dog was never going to leave; I had absolutely, fallen in love with her. I named her Tootsie, Toots for short.

I took her to the vet the following morning to have her checked out, and the vet determined that her back knees were bad and needed metal plates put in for her to walk better. The expensive surgery was scheduled a week later and took about three weeks to heal. The vet felt that she was around fifteen-years-old and that she was part, Shih Tzu. Even though she only weighed six pounds, she was full of life, love, and a little bit of sass.

Toots loved to dance tottering back and forth on her back legs, often danced for food, to go outside or just say hey, how are you. I adored her, and she captured my heart like no other in just a short amount of time. She was such a brave, tough little lady. She would brave any storm to go outside to do her business when the other, larger dogs would wait inside, dry and warm for her to return.

A couple of years later, I noticed that she began to have trouble breathing and had a small seizure. I took her to the vet and found out she was experiencing heart failure, her lungs were filled with fluid. The vet gave her medication to try to relieve her symptoms, and she lasted for about another three weeks. She never recovered and was in a lot of distress. She couldn't stand for long, couldn't lie down for long; she just couldn't do anything to get comfortable, and she couldn't breathe through it all.

I made the truly, heart-wrenching decision to have her put to sleep. I've never had to make this horrible decision before, and I was beyond being consoled. I was there with her, holding her through the rapid process of putting her to sleep. When she lay her head down for the last time, I panicked asking the vet a few times "are you absolutely sure she's gone????" The tears wouldn't stop flowing. I left the vet's office driving aimlessly. I couldn't go home; she was no longer there to greet me. I drove to my work and sat in my car in the parking lot, crying for an hour.

My life felt empty for a long time, but I know that she was loved and she filled my life with so much love, laughter, and light. I felt blessed that we were able to share the rest of her life together. I like to think of her dancing, running and playing across the rainbow bridge. I love you my little Toots.

I would remind anyone who is looking to adopt or rescue an animal that you are making a lifelong commitment. An animal is not temporary or disposable just for the sake of saying you have a pet. You are committing to keeping these pets healthy, and when they get sick, you will financially and physically take care of their health. You will love them, and spend time with them. They are your family. You are their whole world. When you get home from work and they are there to greet you with enthusiasm, take the time to say hello, hold them, and play with them; they have waited for your return all day. If you can't commit, then you shouldn't bring an animal into your family.

Amber McCarty

Toots taught me that taking in a senior dog is one of the most fulfilling things that not only I did in my life, but anyone can do in their life. I will definitely rescue another senior dog; age is just a number, it's the love you can share that matters.

Although we didn't have much time together, every moment we shared made my heart full.

CHADDY NOODY
Minnesota

Original photo of Chaddy Noody was lost in a fire. This rooster was owned by Crystal E. Henze from San Antonio, Texas. Permission was given to use her photo which resembled Chaddy Noody.

1948 – 1948

CHADDY NOODY

It was 1948. My family and I were living in Fergus Falls, Minnesota and I was in the fourth grade. One spring day before Easter, my good friend Nancy Enderson and I were walking home from school and were passing by the Woolworth's Five and Dime Store. In the store window, we saw fluffy, live baby chicks that had been dyed a variety of pastel colors no doubt because Easter was right around the corner. I think the Humane Society eventually put a stop to that practice.

I bought two of the chicks, a pink one, and a blue one, never considering the consequences, or where I'd keep them or what I'd feed them. The blue chick died early on, but the pink one thrived. We didn't know if this one was a boy or girl.

I kept it in a cardboard box in the basement, covered with a screen and a scarf. A light bulb was kept on over the box to keep it warm. I bought a nickel's worth of feed every week from the hatcher. My siblings and I enjoyed holding this soft, small chick. As it grew, the pink fuzz came out and in came the white feathers. Here was this beautiful, majestic looking rooster, a Leghorn (pronounced "Leggern"), which I named Chaddy Noody. I'm not sure how I came up with the name, maybe Chaddy came from the word (chicken), and Noody came from (little), but I can't say for sure. The origins of the Leghorn are not very clear; some breeds came from the Tuscany, Italy area to America around 1828.

Chaddy Noody stayed in our yard most of the time, but sometimes he followed kids home from school and they'd bring him back and say, "Is this your chicken?" He'd chase dogs out of our yard and sometimes climb onto my lap when I sat on the back step hanging his head over my arm and then close his eyes. Chaddy Noody always came to the basement window well in the evening and would wait for me to bring him inside. Mother said he never knew when to crow because it was so dark in the basement.

The day came when I was told by my mother that roosters belonged on a farm, not in a city. Since my grandmother lived on a farm, we would take Chaddy Noody to live there. I was so young at the time; I felt happy and thought it would be best for him. We only had him about three months. My grandmother had a red chicken coop and a lot of hens. After letting him loose in the chicken coop, he realized he was a rooster and not a person. When we came back a couple of weeks later I ran out to greet him, but he chased me away, and my heart was broken. He became so protective of the chickens that he wouldn't let my grandmother into the chicken coop to collect the eggs. Unfortunately, Chaddy Noody had to go; she ate him.

Marcia Olson

Chaddy Noody taught me that even a rooster can be a loving pet, and if you forget who's in charge, bad things can happen.

ABBY

Wisconsin/Minnesota

Abby and Debbie

September 1, 2001 – March 15, 2015

ABBY

Abby was a very special dog that came into our lives when she was almost three years old. The way our lives came together is a bit of a miracle story. It started with my husband Richard's desire to have a dog, specifically a Golden Retriever. He talked many times about wanting to get one, and I was a little resistant because of memories of my childhood dog Tuffy. Tuffy was a wild little Cairn Terrier who barked at everything and loved to escape from our house and to be chased after. I viewed a Golden Retriever as a larger version of that wild little childhood dog. I talked with many of my friends and one of my co-workers, a dog lover, convinced me to go along with my husband's idea to get a dog. I finally agreed to the idea, with one stipulation, no puppy. I had already been through sleepless nights, potty training, and the destruction of my house with two young boys. This led to my decision not to repeat it with a puppy. My husband agreed and together we began the search to find our dog.

The search didn't take long and happened in a way we never expected. We visited my moms' church one Sunday, and following the service, we were sitting together at a table enjoying coffee; a friend of my mom's came up to the table and said, "Something told me I should come over to this table and talk to you about a dog." My mom laughed because she was not a dog lover and she had the same memories of wild little Tuffy. I didn't pay much attention to what was being said until I saw my husband's eyes light up as he asked "What kind of dog?" The woman responded by saying "a Golden Retriever." That got my attention. I heard my husband ask more questions. The woman went on to describe how Abby had come to live with her daughter as a runaway dog and now they were looking for a home for her. My husband then went on to ask when we could meet her. The woman called her daughter Barb, and it was arranged for us to go immediately. We packed up the kids and headed for Hudson, Wisconsin to meet this mystery dog.

Hudson, Wisconsin was about an hour away from our home in Minnesota. So we had a lot of time to talk about the *possibility* of this dog joining our family. I'm the practical one, and my thought was we would meet the dog, learn everything we needed to learn about her, go home, discuss it, and sleep on it before deciding to take the dog. Meanwhile, Richard was envisioning her, dreaming about her, and stated, "I'm in love with her already." This was moving way too fast for me. "How can you love her when you haven't even met her?" I responded. We drove into the driveway of Barb's home, and there was Abby, playing in the front yard with one of her sons. For all of us, it was love at first sight.

Abby was a beautiful, reddish-brown Golden Retriever with a long flowing tail that waved back and forth as she ran to greet us. This was our first experience with a very people oriented dog who came to greet and love every person she met. She bounded towards us and delighted in all the attention she received from my husband, me and our two boys Kris and Jeremy. We were not met with the same delight from Barb's son. We asked the boy if his mother was home and if we could speak with her. Barb came outside and gave us background information on Abby.

ABBY

Abby was originally owned by a couple on a nearby farm. The dog was a purebred Golden Retriever and raised with an older dog, named Peggy. The couple was moving to Arizona and didn't plan on taking the dogs with them. The couple offered to give them away for free to anyone who wanted them. The two dogs were given to some people in town, but the dogs didn't stay long as they escaped and found their way to Barb's house. She tracked down the new owners through the ID tags and returned the dogs. Soon after, the dogs escaped and once again showed up on Barb's doorstep. She felt uneasy about the owners after she returned the dogs previously, so she made a call to the City to inquire about the owners and the dogs. The person on the line warned her not to return the dogs again because they may end up on someone's plate. Apparently, these people had a history of selling dogs for food. She contemplated keeping both dogs along with her two German Shepherds. Barb took Abby and Peggy to the vet for a cleaning and a checkup. The veterinarian informed her of the history of the dogs and their original owners. Barb's family, especially her son Bobby, was very excited about adopting the two new dogs. Unfortunately, one of the German Shepherds did not feel the same way.

Abby and one of the German Shepherds were in constant conflict. Over time the dogs needed to be separated, and the decision to give Abby away was made. Barb's son was very attached to her and was heartbroken about the decision. We assured him we would take good care of her and he was welcome to come and visit her anytime. We also promised updates to his grandma at church. I'm sure Peggy was also saddened to see her longtime companion, Abby, leave.

We packed Abby into our vehicle and headed home. That's when the reality of being new dog owners set in. Our first realization was that we had no idea how to care for a dog and had none of the needed equipment or supplies; we weren't even sure what we needed. Before getting home, we stopped at a Petco in Eden Prairie, Minnesota, about twenty minutes from our house. We were a salesperson's dream customer! We walked in and asked, "What do we need?" Several hundred dollars later we were equipped with a kennel, bed, food, bowls, toys, collar, leash, and owners' manual. We were now ready to start our adventure with our new canine friend. Then a second realization set in. We were leaving in a week for a family trip to Vermont which meant someone was going to need to care for our new dog.

This is when second thoughts about our rushed decision set in. I felt bad about leaving Abby with someone else when she had been bounced back and forth already between multiple homes. Barb and her family offered to take her back for that week, but the thought of ripping Abby away from Barb's son and their dog Peggy a second time was equally painful. Richard offered to stay home and skip the vacation because he didn't want to have to put Abby in a kennel after all she had been through. I wasn't too excited about having our new dog disrupt our vacation plans so I set out to problem solve the best way I knew how; I shared my woes with my friends.

This is also how you find out who your true friends are; they offer to take your dog for a week!

Mary and Rhett were good friends of ours who love Golden Retrievers and owned a couple of them when they lived in rural Wisconsin. They were excited to meet and care for Abby because of their past love and affection for the Goldens. What a blessing this turned out to be. Abby greeted them with the same excitement and warmed up to them instantly. We checked on her frequently while we were gone and everything went well except one accident on the carpet.

When we returned from our trip, Abby was overjoyed to see us. We were equally excited to see her and start our new life together.

One of Abby's favorite things to do was to hang out with us in the basement while we watched television. This became her evening bathing ritual as she'd lick down her whole body. Periodically, she would get up and put her nose under our hand, prompting us to pet her. Every night she would stand by the door to the basement. This was her signal for "basement time." We always felt guilty when we came home late and headed to bed without basement time. That look she gave us always broke our hearts. Sometimes we gave in and went to the basement for a short time because we didn't want to disappoint her.

Abby always wanted to be near us. She rarely wandered away from our sides. When we bought our house, we discovered it came with an electric fence, but we never used it. When we let Abby out, she was often peering in the window waiting for our return. When we went to bed at night she often laid down at the bottom of the stairs since she wasn't allowed upstairs. When we left for the day she laid down next to the door we exited from. I believe she did this to ensure she was right in place for our return. We loved that warm greeting when we came home but sometimes she was a fall hazard and we often tripped over her.

I can't conclude my memories without talking about her tail. She had an amazing tail. It was large and covered with long beautiful flowing hair that reminded me of gold wheat swaying in the wind. She wagged it when she was excited to see someone or even when she was thinking she might see someone. If we were up in the middle of the night, we would hear the thump, thump, thump of her tail without us going downstairs. This was her only skill as a guard dog because she never barked. If there was an intruder, Abby would surely welcome him in with a thump, thump, thump of her tail. Her tail was amazing at dusting furniture and floors as it swept everything she came near. Young children were at risk around her tail because she often knocked them over. Glassware and any other delicate items could not be left unattended or they would soon be sent flying across the room. I realized why Golden Retrievers have hip problems. That mighty tail required the full action of the hips to make it wag. The best part of her tail was the message of joy and love she shared with us every day. I miss that tail and I miss my Abby.

My children also had a wonderful connection with Abby. Often, I heard the complaints about not wanting to walk her, feed her, let her out, and the worst was cleaning off her feet. Despite the chores, our family loved Abby and my sons have strong memories of her as well.

Memories Kris has of Abby.

I remember mom and dad wanting to get a dog, but not a puppy. I was thirteen years old and Abby was full grown. She didn't have to be trained, and she was a lap dog. Dad is the one that really wanted a dog. Mom took her for walks, but it was obvious that she was definitely dad's dog. He was the person who played with her and took her on most of her walks.

I was in the eighth grade when Abby came to live with us. I specifically remember, one of my classmates, Sam, also had a Golden Retriever named Abby and he questioned why we also named our dog Abby. I remember the conversation going something like "hey, we just got a Golden Retriever and her name was already Abby because when we got her, she had a tag with her name on it."

Abby went with us to my grandma's cabin on Pickerel Lake many times. She didn't like to swim even though she knew how and was a great swimmer. She seemed to be scared of the lake and didn't like going into the water. She'd hang out on the dock. One time we visited my aunt and uncle on Potato Lake, and there were ducks swimming out on the water, she ran off the end of the dock and started swimming after them. She was perfectly fine in the water when she wanted, but

I think she just preferred the dock. Dad would sometimes carry her into the lake and she would be nervous, but when there were ducks on the water she ran out and jumped towards them.

When we would go to the lake and take the boat out she would get into the boat and always sat way up in the front to face the wind. She loved when the boat went fast and someone always sat with her to prevent her from falling out. She reminded me of a figurehead on an old wooden sailing ship.

Abby was fine for the most part with other dogs. I think she wanted to be friends with every other canine and if it was a little dog that yipped, she would look at them curiously like…"why are you yipping?" She was also very good with people and just wanted to be petted. Although, I don't think she was a very good guard dog. You could probably come in and take what you wanted as long as you stopped to visit her. She never intentionally barked at people.

My wife, Elyse, remembers my parents saying that when Abby was younger, she may have gotten to close to a fire while sniffing it and possibly singed (damaged) her vocal cords. She definitely could whine and whimper which she did a lot. The only time she actually barked was when something startled her, while dreaming, or if she got hurt when something fell onto her feet or tail. But she never intentionally barked like other dogs.

I know as she got older she didn't have as much energy like she did when she was younger. You could tell she still wanted to do all the same things but couldn't. When she was younger, dad would lift the netting in the back of our SUV and she would jump all the way in. As she got older, she would try to jump in but would end up hopping up a little bit before dad would have to help her get into the truck.

I also remember she wasn't very good at retrieving things. She didn't like to play fetch. You couldn't tell whether she knew how to play fetch and didn't want to or if she didn't get the concept. She liked to chase things and then she would keep it. So you could throw a ball or a toy, and she would run after it, but then she would stay there with the toy as if to say, I have it now, why would I bring it back to you, it's mine.

Abby was a homebody who didn't bolt away at the first chance of freedom. I walked her to the park one time and let her off the leash; I was just sitting there on a bench for a few moments and noticed she disappeared. Most dogs would have run off, Abby decided to head home.

Kris Scott

Memories Jeremy has of Abby.

One memory that always comes to mind is the time Abby ended up eating two presents sent from my aunt and uncle, Diane and Mark. They sent us some artisan chocolates from a local spot in Colorado, but we didn't know as the presents were wrapped. A couple days before Christmas Eve, we came back home from enjoying festivities downtown and saw that both presents were torn open and food scraps were everywhere. We knew Abby had done it, but it took us a moment to realize it was chocolate. I remember getting far more worried than upset, mostly because she had just eaten a load of chocolate. Fortunately, she was OK. We did have to let Diane and Mark know that we never did get to try the chocolate.

Jeremy Scott

Jeremy's memory happened the first Christmas we had Abby. She was a bit on the naughty side as we were trying to adjust to each other and started to train her. She not only got into the candy under the tree but also pulled a plate of Christmas cookies off the counter one evening when we were gone. She ate all the cookies except for the Pepper kaka (a Swedish gingerbread made by my husband's mom, Jean). I'm not sure if she didn't like them or she knew those were my husband's favorite cookie and she left them for him. We will never know for sure.

Abby was a very healthy dog until the last year we had her. She occasionally had episodes of wheezing and gasping for air. The summer before she passed away Jeremy was caring for her while my husband and I were in Washington D.C. for a work-related event. The weather had been very hot and Jeremy took Abby for a walk. As they were returning home, Abby collapsed in the driveway and was gasping for air. I remember the panicked call we received from Jeremy because he didn't know what to do. We told him to relax and bring her inside to cool her off and give her some water. Jeremy responded with, "Easy for you. You're in Washington D.C. having a great time and I'm dealing with a dying dog." Abby recovered from that event but had a few more of those episodes. The vet said this respiratory behavior is common in older dogs and each episode appeared to get worse and worse.

The final episode happened the day Jeremy came home for spring break from the University of Minnesota on March 15, 2015. Jeremy walked into the house and she had one of those attacks. I was over at my mom's place, working on a paper for school when my husband called. He took Abby to the vet and I met him there. The vet gave her something to help ease her breathing but told us these events would continue more frequently and with greater intensity.

We called the boys and let them know what was happening and told them we didn't want Abby to suffer through these spells anymore. The boys were very sad but understanding. Richard and I were with her when the vet gave her the medicine to put her to sleep. She had a very peaceful death as we told her what a good dog she was and that we loved her. We continued to pet her until she breathed her last breath. We were so thankful for the ten and a half years we had her in our lives.

Debbie Scott

ABBY

Abby taught me four important life lessons:

The first lesson was to greet everyone with a positive attitude, she did it with her tail, but I can do it with a smile. The second lesson was to never hold a grudge. Life is too short. Abby never stayed mad or upset, she was always ready for a new adventure. The third lesson was to get some exercise and take a walk. We are still doing this today. The final and most important lesson she taught me was to love your family unconditionally and enjoy your time together.

Animal Shelters and Rescue Leagues

YOU can help make a difference in the lives of animals everywhere. Animals need our help in so many ways as do the shelters themselves. Many are operating on shoe-string budgets. We can all do something, no matter how big or small the gesture.

Check out their volunteer lists and wish lists. There are so many ways you can help:

- Foster or adopt a pet;
- Use your talent to help do a fund-raiser (bake-sales, car washes, a carnival, a garage sale, etc.);
- Donate items needed for the animals;
- Donate items needed for the shelters themselves;
- Give gift cards to shelters for supplies, etc.;
- Money is a huge plus, whatever you can give;
- Volunteer to hold any of the animals, they need that loving human touch;

Animal Shelters and Rescue Leagues

- Volunteer to walk a dog or sit with a cat or other small animal;
- Volunteer to help clean a facility, many hands make light of work.

If you think of something else you can do, let them know.

Find a shelter close to you, contact them and see what they need most, they need your help. Many have Facebook pages on their websites you can click on, go check them out. Go to Amazon Smile, many facilities have a link you can click to help donate; they also have Amazon Wish Lists as well.

All of these facilities are a 501(c) 3 organizations and donations are tax-deductible to the extent of the law.

If we keep waiting for someone else to step up, nothing will get done. These animals need our help. Take the first step, even if it is a little one and contact an animal shelter near you.

If you want to find an animal shelter close to you, simply type on the Google search bar – "animal shelters, (state)". You'll find dozens of animal shelters. Each shelter is listed, their website, phone number and directions. It shows a map of where in the state they are located. See if there is one near you.

Here are just some of the animal shelters I contacted.

Iowa

PAWS & More Animal Shelter
1004 1/2 West Madison Street
Washington, IA 52353
319-653-6713
www.pawsandmorewashington.org
Washingtonpawsandmore1978@gmail.com

Mission Statement: PAWS & More Animal Shelter, also known as Washington County Humane Society, is a private, adoption guarantee shelter located in Washington, Iowa. "PAWS" stands for "Providing Animals with Shelter"; while "More" stands for the loving care and treatment we give to every animal that passes through our doors. We provide humane care to all animals needing protection, seek suitable homes for animals without owners and provide euthanasia when only medically or behaviorally necessary.

Illinois

Heartland Animal Shelter

2975 Milwaukee Ave.
Northbrook, IL 60062
847-296-6400

www.Heartlandanimalshelter.org
info@heartlandanimalshelter.org
heartlandanimals@yahoo.com

Pet Adoption saves 2 lives! The pet you bring home and the pet awaiting a space in the shelter!

Tazewell Animal Protective Society (TAPS)

100 TAPS Lane
Pekin, IL 61554
309-353-8277

www.tapsshelter.org
admin@tapsshelter.org

Kansas

Prairie Paws Animal Shelter

3173 Highway K 68
Ottawa, KS 66067
785-242-2967

http://prairiepaws.org

info@prairiepaws.org

Animal Shelters and Rescue Leagues

Minnesota

Crossroads Animal Shelter

2800 10th St. SE,
Buffalo, MN 55313

763-684-1234

www.crossroadsshelter.org

info@crossroadsshelter.org

Missouri

Rescue-Animals Best Friends

PO Box 493,
Independence, MO 64051
816-254-8664
animalsbestfriends.org
rescue@animalsbestfriends.org

KC Pet Project

contactkcpp@kcmo.org

Main Shelter:

4400 Raytown Rd,
Kansas City, MO 64129
816-513-9821

Zona Rosa:

7351 NW 87th Terrace,
Kansas City, MO 64153
816-587-0224

Petco:

11620 W. 95th St.,
Overland Park, KS 66214
913-438-9740

Check out our Amazon Wish List

Animal Shelters and Rescue Leagues

T.A.R.A. (The Animal Rescue Alliance)

6921 Hunter Street
Raytown, MO 64133
913-710-8237

www.tarasdream.org

Facebook:/theanimalrescuealliance
Twitter: @TARAkcPETrescue
Jenn4tara@gmail.com
email@tarasdream.org

We are primarily foster-based, we do not have a facility that's open to the public, visit our website and donation list, this is a wonderful way to help our homeless pets.

Nebraska

Hearts United for Animals

Box 286,
Auburn, NE 68305
402-274-3679

www.hua.org

hua@hua.org

North Dakota

Circle of Friends Humane Society

4375 North Washington Street
Grand Forks, ND 58203

701-775-3732

www.cofpets.com
lauralee@cofpets.com

Tennessee

White County Animal Shelter

5600 Gum Springs Mountain Road
Sparta, TN 38583
931-761-3647

www.whitecountyanimalshelter.com
wcanimalshelterspartatn@gmail.com

Page Sponsored and Maintained by:
POPS-Pals of The Pooches at
The White County Animal Shelter

Check them out.

Morristown Hamblen Human Society

300 Dice Street,
Morristown, TN 37813
423-581-1494

Mh-humanesociety.com
Mhhsanimals@gmail.com

"Remember, one person may not be able to change the world, but one person can change the life of an adopted animal forever!" Dr. Michael Bratton, President of the Board of Morristown Hamblen Humane Society

ANIMAL SHELTERS AND RESCUE LEAGUES

Washington

Yakima Humane Society

2405 West Birchfield Road
Yakima, WA 98901
509-457-6854

Founded 1904

www.yakimahumane.org
information@yakimahumane.org

Pet Loss Resources

Listed below are a few pet loss resources. Pet loss support groups to euthanasia at home instead of a pet clinic or hospital to creative ways to remember your pet and the loving special bond you had and shared with them.

They just don't understand!

The death of a beloved pet can be profound and life-changing, in ways that outsiders often don't "get".

You will find helpful information and gentle support here:

Recover-from-grief.com

https://www.recover-from-grief.com/pet-death.html

www.petlossathome.com   Pet Loss At home is a business that helps "make a difficult time in losing a pet a bit better by being surrounded by the comfort of home." We are 100 vets across the country helping with home euthanasia and our website is full of helpful tips for any pet owner during end-of-life. We do not cover all counties in the U.S., but we do cover about 25% of the U.S. population in most major cities. See also our Pet Loss Support Group.

Celebrating the unique bond between animals of all species, ages, and lifestyles and their human families.

Visit our Pet Loss Support Group

www.humananimalbondtrust.org

info@humananimalbondtrust.org

a 501(c)(3) non-profit organization

303-539-7646

WE HAD A SIMPLE DREAM . . . to create a one-of-a-kind healing place to bring comfort to those who are grieving the loss of their pets.

We are not a traditional memorial site. Instead we specialize in creating an interactive experience designed to foster and nurture the loving eternal bond you share with your beloved pet. For a more personal experience, many features throughout our site are personalized with your pet's name including our unique rainbow bridge carriage tour experience for you and your pet. Other features include articles, personalized rainbow bridge poems, candle lighting, Monday candle ceremonies and more.

https://www.justovertherainbowbridge.com/

239-216-4822

Can you see your story in my next book?

Let me know and I'll send you my simple guideline sheet.

You can email me at:

Tmtpetstories18@gmail.com

About The Author

Trish Titus is originally from west central Iowa. Her writing started shortly after the loss of her beloved cat, Delilah. She has given grief-stricken pet owners the opportunity to share their stories.

When not writing, she likes to sew, travel, read, and spend time with her daughter and son-in-law.

If you have a story to share, Trish would love to hear from you. You can reach her at Tmtpetstories18@gmail.com.

Thoughts and Memory Pages

Thoughts and Memory Pages

Delilah and Others Like Her

Thoughts and Memory Pages

www.ingramcontent.com/pod-product-compliance
Lightning Source LLC
Chambersburg PA
CBHW071242070526
44583CB00017B/2291